GRADES
K-2

the Super Source™
Cuisenaire® Rods

D1550858

Cuisenaire Company of America, Inc.
White Plains, NY

Cuisenaire extends its warmest thanks to the many teachers and students across the country who helped ensure the success of the Super Source™ series by participating in the outlining, writing, and field testing of the materials.

Project Director: Judith Adams
Managing Editor: Doris Hirschhorn
Editorial Team: Patricia Kijak Anderson, Linda Dodge, John Nelson, Deborah J. Slade, Harriet Slonim
Field Test Coordinator: Laurie Verdeschi

Design Manager: Phyllis Aycock
Text Design: Amy Berger, Tracey Munz
Line Art and Production: Joan Lee, Fiona Santoianni
Cover Design: Michael Muldoon
Illustrations: Rebecca Thornburgh

the Super Source™
Table of Contents

Using the Super Source™

The Super Source™ is a series of books each of which contains a collection of activities to use with a specific math manipulative. Driving **the Super Source**™ is Cuisenaire's conviction that children construct their own understandings through rich, hands-on mathematical experiences. Although the activities in each book are written for a specific grade range, they all connect to the core of mathematics learning that is important to every K-6 child. Thus, the material in many activities can easily be refocused for children at other grade levels. Because the activities are not arranged sequentially, children can work on any activity at any time.

The lessons in **the Super Source**™ all follow a basic structure consistent with the vision of mathematics teaching described in the *Curriculum and Evaluation Standards for School Mathematics* published by the National Council of Teachers of Mathematics.

All of the activities in this series involve Problem Solving, Communication, Reasoning, and Mathematical Connections—the first four NCTM Standards. Each activity also focuses on one or more of the following curriculum strands: Number, Geometry, Measurement, Patterns/Functions, Probability/Statistics, Logic.

HOW LESSONS ARE ORGANIZED

At the beginning of each lesson, you will find, to the right of the title, both the major curriculum strands to which the lesson relates and the particular topics that children will work with. Each lesson has three main sections. The first, GETTING READY, offers an *Overview*, which states what children will be doing, and why, and a list of "What You'll Need." Specific numbers of Cuisenaire Rods are suggested on this list but can be adjusted as the needs of your specific situation dictate. Before an activity, rods can be counted out and placed in containers or self-sealing plastic bags for easy distribution. When crayons are called for, it is understood that their colors are those that match the Cuisenaire Rods and that markers may be used in place of crayons. Blackline masters that are provided for your convenience at the back of the book are referenced on this list. Paper, pencils, scissors, tape, and materials for making charts, which are necessary in certain activities, are usually not.

Although overhead Cuisenaire Rods and the suggestion to make overhead transparencies of the blackline masters are always listed in "What You'll Need" as optional, these materials are highly effective when you want to demonstrate the use of Cuisenaire Rods. As you move the rods on the screen, children can work with the same materials at their seats. Children can also use the overhead to present their work to other members of their group or to the class.

The second section, THE ACTIVITY, first presents a possible scenario for *Introducing* the children to the activity. The aim of this brief introduction is to help you give children the tools they will need to investigate independently. However, care has been taken to avoid undercutting the activity itself. Since these investigations are designed to enable children to increase their own mathematical power, the idea is to set the stage but not steal the show! The heart of the lesson, *On Their Own*, is found in a box at the top of the second page of each lesson. Here, rich problems stimulate many different problem-solving approaches and lead to a variety of solutions. These hands-on explorations have the potential for bringing children to new mathematical ideas and deepening skills.

On Their Own is intended as a stand-alone activity for children to explore with a partner or in a small group. Be sure to make the needed directions clearly visible. You may want to write them on the chalkboard or on an overhead or present them either on reusable cards or paper. For children who may have difficulty reading the directions, you can read them aloud or make sure that at least one "reader" is in each group.

The last part of this second section, *The Bigger Picture*, gives suggestions for how children can share their work and their thinking and make mathematical connections. Class charts and children's recorded work provide a springboard for discussion. Under "Thinking and Sharing," there are several prompts that you can use to promote discussion. Children will not be able to respond to these prompts with one-word answers. Instead, the prompts encourage children to describe what they notice, tell how they found their results, and give the reasoning behind their answers. Thus children learn to verify their own results rather than relying on the teacher to determine if an answer is "right" or "wrong." Though the class discussion might immediately follow the investigation, it is important not to cut the activity short by having a class discussion too soon.

The Bigger Picture often includes a suggestion for a "Writing" (or drawing) assignment. This is meant to help children process what they have just been doing. You might want to use these ideas as a focus for daily or weekly entries in a math journal that each child keeps.

I machtied the colored shapes with the shapes on the board. It didn't matter order I put them in.

From: *Rod Lotto*

If I put down one wrong one the other player will porbobly put down one that will fors me two land on the thirteen.

From: *Thirteen is Out!*

The Bigger Picture always ends with ideas for "Extending the Activity." Extensions take the essence of the main activity and either alter or extend its parameters. These activities are well used with a class that becomes deeply involved in the primary activity or for children who finish before the others. In any case, it is probably a good idea to expose the entire class to the possibility of, and the results from, such extensions.

The third and final section of the lesson is TEACHER TALK. Here, in *Where's the Mathematics?*, you can gain insight into the underlying mathematics of the activity and discover some of the strategies children are apt to use as they work. Solutions are also given—when such are necessary and/or helpful. Because *Where's the Mathematics?* provides a view of what may happen in the lesson as well as the underlying mathematical potential that may grow out of it, this may be the section that you want to read before presenting the activity to children.

USING THE ACTIVITIES

The Super Source™ has been designed to fit into the variety of classroom environments in which it will be used. These range from a completely manipulative-based classroom to one in which manipulatives are just beginning to play a part. You may choose to use some activities in **the Super Source**™ in the way set forth in each lesson (introducing an activity to the whole class, then breaking the class up into groups that all work on the same task, and so forth). You will then be able to circulate among the groups as they work to observe and perhaps comment on each child's work. This approach requires a full classroom set of materials but allows you to concentrate on the variety of ways that children respond to a given activity.

Alternatively, you may wish to make two or three related activities available to different groups of children at the same time. You may even wish to use different manipulatives to explore the same mathematical concept. (Color Tiles and Snap™ Cubes, for example, can be used to teach some of the same concepts as Cuisenaire Rods.) This approach does not require full classroom sets of a particular manipulative. It also permits greater adaptation of materials to individual children's needs and/or preferences.

If children are comfortable working independently, you might want to set up a "menu"—that is, set out a number of related activities from which children can choose. Children should be encouraged to write about their experiences with these independent activities.

However you choose to use **the Super Source**™ activities, it would be wise to allow time for several groups or the entire class to share their experiences. The dynamics of this type of interaction, in which children share not only solutions and strategies but also feelings and intuitions, is the basis of continued mathematical growth. It allows children who are beginning to form a mathematical structure to clarify it and those who have mastered just isolated concepts to begin to see how these concepts might fit together.

Again, both the individual teaching style and combined learning styles of the children should dictate the specific method of utilizing **the Super Source**™ lessons. At first sight, some activities may appear too difficult for some of your children, and you may find yourself tempted to actually "teach" by modeling exactly how an activity can lead to a particular learning outcome. If you do this, you rob children of the chance to try the activity in whatever way they can. As long as children have a way to begin an investigation, give them time and opportunity to see it through. Instead of making assumptions about what children will or won't do, watch and listen. The excitement and challenge of the activity—as well as the chance to work cooperatively—may bring out abilities in children that will surprise you.

If you are convinced, however, that an activity does not suit your students, adjust it, by all means. You may want to change the language, either by simplifying it or by referring to specific vocabulary that you and your children already use and are comfortable with. On the other hand, if you suspect that an activity is not challenging enough, you may want to read through the activity extensions for a variation that you can give children instead.

RECORDING

Although the direct process of working with Cuisenaire Rods is a valuable one, it is afterward, when children look at, compare, share, and think about their work, that an activity yields its greatest rewards. However, because Cuisenaire Rod designs can't always be left intact, children need an effective way to record their work. The "What You'll Need" listing at the beginning of each lesson often specifies the kind of recording paper to use. For example, it seems natural for children to record Cuisenaire Rod patterns on 1-centimeter grid paper. Children might duplicate their work on centimeter grid paper, coloring in boxes on grids that exactly match the rods in size. You may want to have younger children record their work on 2-centimeter grid paper, either to reflect the actual size of the jumbo Cuisenaire Rods that they are working with or merely to provide them with larger areas to color. Older children may be able to use grids with boxes that are smaller than 1-centimeter or may even use a Cuisenaire Rod template to reproduce each piece in the design.

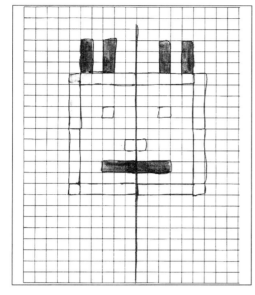

From: *Mirror Monster*

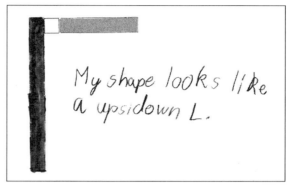

From: *Make a Match!*

Cuisenaire Rods are referred to by the following standard notation:

w = **w**hite	**y** = **y**ellow	**n** = brow**n**
r = **r**ed	**d** = **d**ark green	**e** = blue
g = light **g**reen	**k** = blac**k**	*o* = **o**range
p = **p**urple		

Children often make use of such coding or create their own to describe the relationships they have discovered through the use of the Cuisenaire Rods.

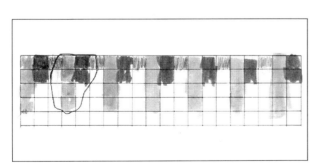

From: *Copy and Repeat*

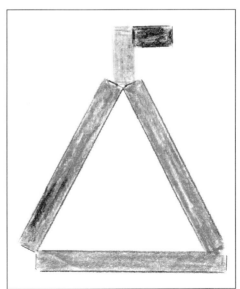

From: *Build a Boat*

Another interesting way to "freeze" a Cuisenaire Rod design is to create it using a software piece, and then get a printout. Children can use a classroom or resource-room computer if it is available or, where possible, extend the activity into a home assignment by utilizing their home computers.

Recording involves more than copying designs. Writing, drawing, and making charts and tables are also ways to record. By creating a table of data gathered in the course of their investigations, children are able to draw conclusions and look for patterns. When children write or draw, either in their group or later by themselves, they are clarifying their understanding of their recent mathematical experience.

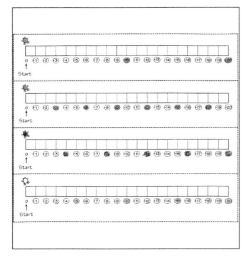

From: *Jumping Frogs*

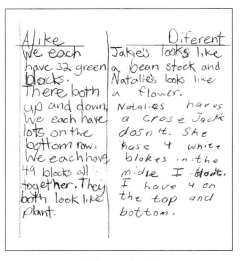

From: *Alike and Different*

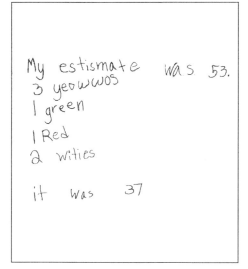

From: *Build a Boat*

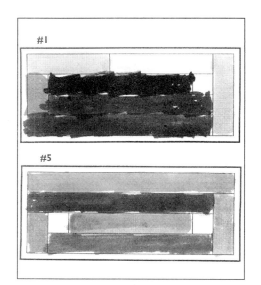

From: *Rod Lotto*

With a roomful of children busily engaged in their investigations, it is not easy for a teacher to keep track of how individual children are working. Having tangible material to gather and examine when the time is right will help you to keep in close touch with each child's learning.

Exploring Cuisenaire® Rods

Cuisenaire Rods are a versatile collection of rectangular rods of ten colors, each color corresponding to a different length. The shortest rod, the white, is one centimeter long; the longest, the orange, is ten centimeters long. One set of rods contains 74 rods: 4 each of the orange (O), blue (e), brown (n), black (k), dark green (d), and yellow (y); 6 purple (p); 10 light green (g); 12 red (r); and 22 white (w). One special aspect of the rods is that, when they are arranged in order of length in a pattern commonly called a "staircase," each rod differs from the next by 1 centimeter, the length of the shortest rod, the white.

Unlike Color Tiles, which provide a discrete model of numbers, Cuisenaire Rods, because of their different, related lengths, provide a continuous model. Thus, they allow you to assign a value to one rod and then assign values to the other rods by using the relationships among the rods.

Cuisenaire Rods can be used to develop a wide variety of mathematical ideas at many different levels of complexity. Initially, however, children use the rods to explore spatial relationships by making flat designs that lie on a table or by making three-dimensional designs by

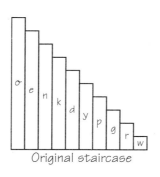
Original staircase

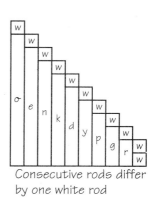
Consecutive rods differ by one white rod

stacking the rods. The intent of children's designs, whether to cover a certain amount of a table top or to fill a box, will lead children to discover how some combinations of rods are equal in length to other, single rods. Children's designs can also provide a context for investigating symmetry. Older children who have no previous experience with Cuisenaire Rods may explore by comparing and ordering the lengths of the rods and then recording the results on grid paper to visualize the inherent "structure" of the design. In all their early work with the rods, children have a context in which to develop their communication skills through the use of grade-appropriate arithmetic and geometric vocabulary.

Though children need to explore freely, some may appreciate specific challenges, such as being asked to make designs with certain types of symmetry, or certain characteristics, such as different colors representing different fractional parts.

WORKING WITH CUISENAIRE RODS

One of the basic uses of Cuisenaire Rods is to provide a model for the numbers 1 to 10. If the white rod is assigned the value of 1, the red rod is assigned the value of 2 because the red rod has the same length as a "train" of two white rods. Similarly, the rods from light green through orange are assigned values from 3 through 10, respectively. The orange and white rods can provide a model for place value. To find the length of a certain train, children can cover the train with as many orange rods as they can and then fill in the remaining distance with white rods; so a train covered with 3 orange rods and 4 white rods is 34 white rods long.

The rods can be placed end-to-end to model addition. For example, 2 + 3 can be found by first making a train with a red rod (2) and a light green rod (3) and then finding the single rod (yellow) whose length (5) is equal in length to the two-car train. This model corresponds to addition on a number line.

The rods can also be used for acting out subtraction as the search for a missing addend. For example, 5 – 2 can be found by placing a red rod (2) on top of a yellow (5), then looking for the rod which, when placed next to the red, makes a train equal in length to the yellow.

Multiplication, such as 5 x 2, is interpreted as repeated addition by making a train of five red rods or of two yellow rods.

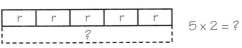

Division, such as 10 ÷ 2, may be interpreted as repeated subtraction ("How many red rods make a train as long as an orange rod?") or as sharing ("Two of what color rod make a train as long as an orange rod?").

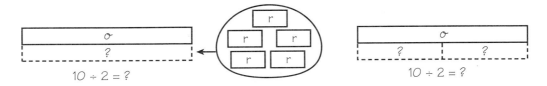

Cuisenaire Rods also make effective models for decimals and fractions. If the orange rod is designated as the unit rod, then the white, red, and light green rods represent 0.1, 0.2, and 0.3, respectively. If the dark green rod is chosen as the unit, then the white, red, and light green rods represent $\frac{1}{6}$, $\frac{2}{6}$ ($\frac{1}{3}$), and $\frac{3}{6}$ ($\frac{1}{2}$), respectively. Once the unit rod has been established, addition, subtraction, multiplication, and division of decimals and fractions can be modeled in the same way as are the operations with whole numbers.

Cuisenaire Rods are suitable for a variety of geometric and measurement investigations. Once children develop a sense that the white rod is one centimeter long, they have little difficulty in accepting and using centimeters as units of length. Since the face of the white rod has an area of one square centimeter, the rods are ideal for finding area in square centimeters. Since the volume of the white rod is one cubic centimeter, the rods can exemplify the meaning of volume as children use rods to fill up boxes. Children may even develop a sense of a milliliter as the capacity of a container that holds exactly one white rod.

Cuisenaire Rods offer many possibilities for forming and discovering number patterns both through creating designs that are growing according to some pattern and through finding the number of ways in which a rod can be made as the sum of other rods. This second scenario can lead to the concept of factors of a number and prime numbers.

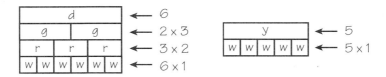

The rods also provide a context for the building of logical reasoning skills. For example, children can use two loops of string to create a Venn Diagram showing the multiples of both red and light green rods (which represent 2 and 3, respectively) by placing the multiples of red (red, purple, dark green, brown, and orange) in one loop, the multiples of light green (light green, dark green, and blue) in the other loop, and then creating an overlap of the two loops and placing the rod representing the common multiple (dark green which represents 6) in the overlap.

ASSESSING CHILDREN'S UNDERSTANDING

Cuisenaire Rods are wonderful tools for assessing children's mathematical thinking. Watching children work with Cuisenaire Rods gives you a sense of how they approach a mathematical problem. Their thinking can be "seen," in so far as that thinking is expressed through the way they construct, recognize, and continue spatial patterns. When a class breaks up into small working groups, you are able to circulate, listen, and raise questions, all the while focusing on how individuals are thinking. Here is a perfect opportunity for authentic assessment.

Having children describe their designs and share their strategies and thinking with the whole class gives you another opportunity for observational assessment. Furthermore, you may want to gather children's recorded work or invite them to choose pieces to add to their math portfolios.

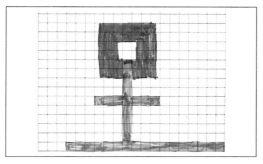
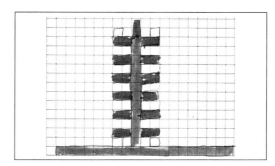

From: *Alike and Different*

Models of teachers assessing children's understanding can be found in Cuisenaire's series of videotapes listed below.

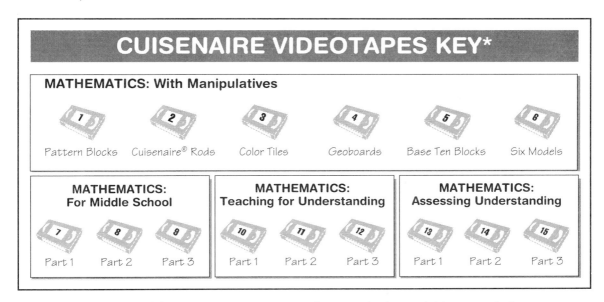

*See *Overview of the Lessons*, pages 16-17, for specific lesson/video correlation.

Connect
the Super Source™
to NCTM Standards.

	PROBLEM SOLVING	COMMUNICATION	REASONING	CONNECTIONS	Geometry	Logic	Measurement	Number	Patterns/Functions	Probability/Statistics
ALIKE AND DIFFERENT	◆	◆	◆	◆				◆		
BANK-5!	◆	◆	◆	◆				◆		◆
BUILD A BOAT	◆	◆	◆	◆			◆	◆		
CHALLENGE MATCH	◆	◆	◆	◆		◆		◆		
COPY AND REPEAT	◆	◆	◆	◆					◆	
COVER THE GIRAFFE	◆	◆	◆	◆	◆	◆	◆			
HOW MANY TWO-CAR TRAINS?	◆	◆	◆	◆				◆	◆	
JUMPING FROGS	◆	◆	◆	◆				◆		
LOAD THE TRUCKS!	◆	◆	◆	◆				◆		◆
MAKE A MATCH!	◆	◆	◆	◆		◆				
MIRROR MONSTER	◆	◆	◆	◆	◆					
MYSTERY TRAINS	◆	◆	◆	◆		◆		◆		
ROD LOTTO	◆	◆	◆	◆			◆	◆		
ROD SQUEEZE	◆	◆		◆				◆		
ROD TOYS	◆	◆	◆	◆	◆			◆		
SIDES OF A TRIANGLE	◆	◆	◆	◆	◆			◆		
THIRTEEN IS OUT!	◆	◆	◆	◆		◆		◆		
WHAT'S IN A SCOOP?	◆	◆	◆	◆		◆		◆		◆

Correlate *the Super Source*™ to your curriculum.

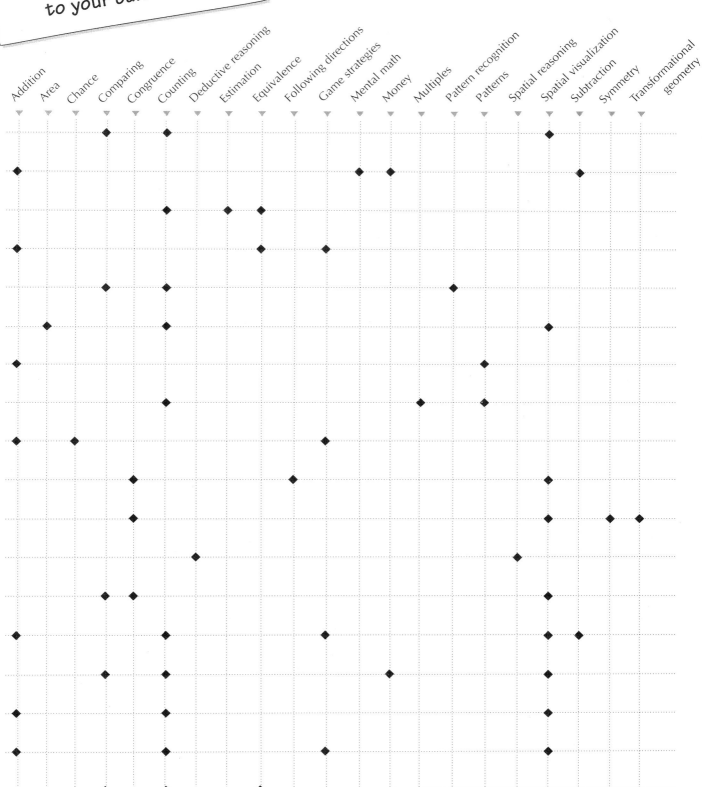

Classroom-tested activities contained in these *Super Source™* Cuisenaire Rods books focus on the math strands in the charts below.

...the *Super Source*™ Cuisenaire® Rods, Grades 3-4

Geometry	Logic	Measurement
Number	Patterns/Functions	Probability/Statistics

...the *Super Source*™ Cuisenaire® Rods, Grades 5-6

Geometry	Logic	Measurement
Number	Patterns/Functions	Probability/Statistics

Classroom-tested activities contained in these *Super Source*™ books focus on the math strands as indicated in these charts.

the Super Source™ Tangrams, Grades K-2

Geometry	Logic	Measurement
Number	**Patterns/Functions**	**Probability/Statistics**

the Super Source™ Color Tiles, Grades K-2

Geometry	Logic	Measurement
Number	**Patterns/Functions**	**Probability/Statistics**

the Super Source™ Geoboards, Grades K-2

Geometry	Logic	Measurement
Number	**Patterns/Functions**	**Probability/Statistics**

the Super Source™ Snap™ Cubes, Grades K-2

Geometry	Logic	Measurement
Number	**Patterns/Functions**	**Probability/Statistics**

the Super Source™ Pattern Blocks, Grades K-2

Geometry	Logic	Measurement
Number	**Patterns/Functions**	**Probability/Statistics**

Overview of the Lessons

Comparing, Counting, Spatial visualization

Children make shapes from Cuisenaire Rods of their own choosing. Then they
compare their shapes and discuss how the shapes are alike and how they are different.

Addition, Subtraction, Money, Mental math

Using white, yellow, and orange Cuisenaire Rods to represent pennies, nickels,
and dimes respectively, children find and compare the different amounts that can
result from groups of five "rod-coins."

Equivalence, Counting, Estimation

Children make "boats" using Cuisenaire Rods and then estimate how many white
rods are needed to cover the shape of their boat.

Equivalence, Addition, Game strategies

In this game for two players, children take turns matching two-car Cuisenaire Rod
trains to a single rod in an effort to be the last to make a two-car train.

Pattern recognition, Counting, Comparing

Children use Cuisenaire Rods to form patterns by repeating given designs. They
then determine the number of rods in the patterns.

Counting, Area, Spatial visualization

Children cover the outline of a giraffe using a specified set of Cuisenaire Rods.
They compare their work and try to identify as many different solutions as possible.

Addition, Patterns

Children select Cuisenaire Rods, then find and record the two-car trains whose
lengths match the selected rods.

Patterns, Counting, Multiples

Pretending that a Cuisenaire Rod of a chosen color is a jumping frog, children
move the rod along a number line. They then compare the "jumps" taken by several "frogs."

Addition, Chance, Game strategies

In this game for two players, children take turns spinning one of two spinners in order to
collect enough Cuisenaire Rods to fill four trucks, each of which carries a 10-centimeter-
long "load."

See video key, page 11.

Cuisenaire Rods, Grades K-2

 See video key, page 11.

ALIKE AND DIFFERENT

Getting Ready

What You'll Need

Cuisenaire Rods, 1 set per pair
Overhead Cuisenaire Rods (optional)

Overview

Children make shapes from Cuisenaire Rods of their own choosing. Then they compare their shapes and discuss how the shapes are alike and how they are different. In this activity, children have the opportunity to:

◆ recognize how shapes can be described in relation to other shapes

◆ understand the meanings of *alike* and *different*

◆ develop and use language related to geometry concepts

The Activity

Introducing

◆ Display this arrangement of Cuisenaire Rods.

◆ Tell children to take three of the same rods. Ask them to use these rods to make a new shape that is like yours in some way yet different from it in another way.

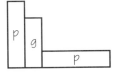

◆ Invite volunteers to share their new shapes, describing how each is like the shape you modeled and how it is different.

◆ Create a new arrangement of rods and have children repeat the activity until you feel that children are ready for *On Their Own*.

On Their Own

> How can a Cuisenaire Rod shape that you make be the same as a shape your partner makes? How can these shapes be different?
>
> - Work with a partner. Each of you take groups of the same Cuisenaire Rods. Use your rods to make a shape that you like.
>
> - Put your shape next to your partner's. Look at both shapes carefully.
>
> - Talk to your partner about the ways your shapes are alike. Talk about how they are different from one another.
>
> - Find a way to record your shapes.
>
> - Set up a chart like this. Work together to fill the chart with words that tell about your shapes.
>
> | How Our Shapes Are... | |
> |---|---|
> | Alike | Different |
> | | |
>
> - Be ready to share your shapes and your chart.

The Bigger Picture

Thinking and Sharing

Invite a pair to post their recordings side by side. Then ask them to read their charts. Ask the other children if they can suggest additional likenesses and differences.

Use prompts such as these to promote class discussion:

- ◆ What did you notice first about your shape and your partner's?

- ◆ Are any pairs' shapes exactly alike? Are any almost alike? How?

- ◆ Would any of the posted shapes become exactly alike if some of the colors were exchanged? Explain.

- ◆ How are all the posted shapes alike? Are they all different in any way? How?

Extending the Activity

Have children do the activity again, but this time have them build their shapes from a specific number of Cuisenaire Rods.

Where's the Mathematics?

This open-ended activity stresses both oral and written communication in mathematics. Children can choose the color of the rods and the number of rods, then use them to create shapes limited only by their imagination. As partners compare their two shapes, the process of writing down similarities and differences forces children to think about what they see and leads them to notice small distinctions. Later, when children listen to the lists of likenesses and differences, they may be alerted to different ways of describing those that they observed in their own work.

Many children will begin their lists by noting likenesses, making comments such as "have the same color" and "use the same number of rods." After that, they note the differences, which are likely to form a much longer column. Some children will use their rods to create recognizable shapes, such as houses and boats, while other children will create free-form imaginary shapes.

Children begin to realize how much there is to say about even the simplest shape as they hear descriptive words and phrases that relate to lengths of sides, types of angles, area, slant of the lines, numbers of sides and angles, and so on. Children's charts may include words of comparison, such as *bigger, smaller, taller, longer,* and *wider.* Charts are also likely to include words and phrases indicating direction, such as *on the right, at the top, underneath,* and *above.* Making the lists will help children see how the use of precise language improves communication.

Children are apt to do a fair amount of counting as they find the number of sides and angles for each shape. As they record this kind of information on their charts, children can begin to see the value of numbers as descriptors. Be on the lookout for children who may confuse the number of rods used to make the shape with the number of sides of the shape. For example, this figure has four sides but children may mistakenly think it has five, since the bottom is composed of two rods.

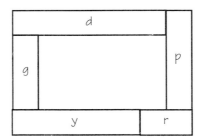

Children may be surprised to see how different two shapes with the same number of sides can look. The orientation and right angles in this trapezoid make it appear quite different from the rectangle shown on the previous page.

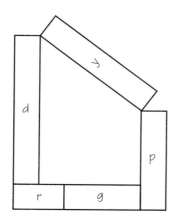

As a pre-assessment tool, you can use this lesson to learn what children already know about shapes and geometric terms. For instance, they might use the term "square corners" to describe right angles or "has four sides" to describe a rectangle. On the other hand, you can use this lesson as a post-assessment tool for checking children's use of the precise geometric terms that you have been using in class.

BANK-5!

- Addition
- Subtraction
- Money
- Mental math

Getting Ready

What You'll Need

Cuisenaire Rods, white, yellow, and orange rods from 2 sets per pair

Bank-5! spinner, 1 per pair, page 90

Piggy Bank worksheet, 1 per child, page 91

Overhead Cuisenaire Rods and/or *Piggy Bank* worksheet transparency (optional)

Overview

Using white, yellow, and orange Cuisenaire Rods to represent pennies, nickels, and dimes respectively, children find and compare the different amounts that can result from groups of five "rod-coins." In this activity, children have the opportunity to:

- ◆ do computation
- ◆ explore how the design of a spinner affects their results
- ◆ internalize the relationship between pennies, nickels, and dimes

The Activity

You may wish to line up five pennies next to the nickel and two nickels and/or ten pennies next to the dime to reinforce children's understanding of equivalent values.

Introducing

- ◆ Display a penny, a nickel, and a dime. Have children name the coins and identify the value of each.
- ◆ Tell children to pretend that Cuisenaire Rods are coins and to think of the white rod as a penny.
- ◆ Invite volunteers to determine which rod they could think of as a nickel.
- ◆ Explain that the yellow rod is the most logical choice for a nickel. Line up five white rods next to a yellow rod to show this.
- ◆ Now ask children to suggest which rod should be a dime.
- ◆ Line up 10 white rods, then two yellow rods, next to an orange rod to show that the orange should be the dime.

On Their Own

How much can 5 "rod-coins" be worth?

- Work with a partner. Pretend that the white, yellow, and orange Cuisenaire Rods are rod-coins. Here's what they are worth:

    1 white rod = 1 penny, or 1¢
    1 yellow rod = 1 nickel, or 5¢
    1 orange rod = 1 dime, or 10¢

- Take turns spinning a spinner that looks like this.

- For each spin, put a matching rod on your Piggy Bank worksheet. Stop after you both have 5 rods in your Piggy Banks.

- Now find out how much money you each saved. Record these amounts. Circle the greater amount.

- Empty your piggy banks! Do the activity 2 more times.

- Be ready to talk about what you noticed.

The Bigger Picture

Thinking and Sharing

Invite children to tell the amount of money they were able to save in one game and then challenge the other children to figure out which rod-coins must have been collected. For example, if the first child volunteers that she saved 22¢, the rest of the children can use their rod-coins to figure out that 1 dime, 2 nickels, and 2 pennies were collected. On the chalkboard, begin a list that looks like this:

22¢ — 1 dime, 2 nickels, 2 pennies

Use prompts such as these to promote class discussion:

- What do you notice about our list?
- What was the least amount anyone saved on five spins? Do you think it is possible to save less?
- What was the greatest amount anyone saved on five spins? Do you think it is possible to save more?
- Is it possible to spin all the amounts between the least and greatest amounts? Explain.
- Did you spin one rod-coin more often than the others? If so, why do you think it happened?

Writing

Have children describe at least three different ways to save 35¢. For each way, ask children to figure out how many spins would be needed.

Extending the Activity

1. Have children repeat the activity. This time, after five spins, have each pair figure out the difference in the amounts they each saved.

2. Prepare an outline of a spinner divided into thirds. Mark the sections "1¢, 5¢," and "10¢." Display the spinner. Invite children to predict how the amount of savings they might have using this spinner (with sections of equal size) might differ from the amounts they had using the original spinner (with sections of unequal size). Allow them to try the activity using this spinner to check their predictions.

Teacher Talk

Where's the Mathematics?

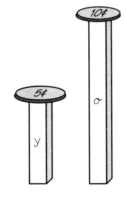

This activity gives children experience working with money concepts. The *On Their Own* activity focuses on collecting and counting change. Children have an opportunity to reflect on the different amounts of money that may be made from a combination of five coins if the coins are limited only to pennies, nickels, and dimes.

Children often have a difficult time counting money. Frequently the difficulty arises from the fact that the relative sizes of the coins do not reflect their relative values. The smallest coin, the dime, is worth the most! A nickel certainly does not look five times larger than a penny yet the value of the nickel is five times the value of a penny. Using Cuisenaire Rods to represent pennies, nickels, and dimes may help children make the connection between each coin and its relative value since five white rods are equivalent to a yellow rod and 2 yellow rods are equivalent to an orange rod. The lengths of the rods do reflect their relative money values in the game. You may even wish to tape actual nickels and dimes or paper facsimilies of the coins to the rods for some children. (Since a penny is larger than a white rod, it would be cumbersome to tape a penny to that rod.)

As the children volunteer the amounts of money they collected and the rest of the class tries to figure out the coins that were collected, they will be finding many of the entries on this table:

Possible to Save	Pennies	Nickels	Dimes
5¢	5	0	0
9¢	4	1	0
13¢	3	2	0
14¢	4	0	1
17¢	2	3	0
18¢	3	1	1
21¢	1	4	0

3. Use this activity to focus on probability. Have each child spin the original spinner ten times, tallying each spin as shown in the example to the right. Create a class chart of all the results.

1¢	~~||||~~	
5¢			
10¢			

4. Tell children to play the game again, this time collecting six coins instead of five. Compile some of their results in a class chart showing which amounts could be collected and which six coins would be needed for each amount.

Possible to Save	Pennies	Nickels	Dimes
22¢	2	2	1
23¢	3	0	2
25¢	0	5	0
26¢	1	3	1
27¢	2	1	2
30¢	0	4	1
31¢	1	2	2
32¢	2	0	3
35¢	0	3	2
36¢	1	1	3
40¢	0	2	3
41¢	1	0	4
45¢	0	1	4
50¢	0	0	5

Not all of these amounts may occur when your class plays the game. The design of the spinner makes some amounts more likely to occur than others. For example, it is possible—but not very likely—that a child would spin a dime five times in a row. Probing with questions, such as "Do you think it is possible to save more?" and "Is it possible to spin all the amounts between the least and greatest amounts?" will encourage children to think about possible amounts that may not have actually occurred while the game was played.

Discussing what actually happened in the game versus what could have happened will help children distinguish between the words *probable* and *possible*, which will give them a headstart in understanding important probability concepts.

BUILD A BOAT

- Equivalence
- Counting
- Estimation

Getting Ready

What You'll Need

Cuisenaire Rods, 1 set per pair

1-centimeter grid paper, page 110

Overhead Cuisenaire Rods and/or
1-centimeter grid paper transparency
(optional)

Overview

Children make "boats" using Cuisenaire Rods and then estimate how many white rods are needed to cover the shape of their boat. In this activity, children have the opportunity to:

◆ discover numerical relationships among the rods

◆ develop strategies for adding

The Activity

Introducing

◆ Ask children how many white rods would be needed to exactly cover a yellow rod.

◆ Elicit that five white rods would be needed to cover the yellow rod.

◆ Now make a train of two yellow rods. Ask how many white rods would exactly cover this two-car train.

◆ Have a volunteer use white rods to verify that ten of them are needed to cover the two-car train.

w	w	w	w	w	w	w	w	w	w
y					y				

On Their Own

How many white Cuisenaire Rods would you need to build a boat?

- Work with a partner. Build a boat according to these rules:
    - Use at least 5 rods, but no more than 10.
    - Make the boat lie flat.
    - Use any colors except white.
- Estimate how many white rods would cover the rods of your boat.
- Check your estimate by figuring out the exact number of white rods that would be needed. Find 2 ways to do this.
- Record how many of each color rod you used in your boat. Record the total number of white rods.
- Leave your boat in place. Be ready to talk about what you did.

The Bigger Picture

Thinking and Sharing

Invite children to look at everyone's boats before beginning the discussion. Then, have them to gather around each pair's work as the children describe their boat.

Use prompts like these to promote class discussion:

- How did you check your estimate? Explain.
- Which way of finding the exact number of white rods do you like the best?
- Which boat needed the least number of white rods? Which boat needed the greatest number?
- Did any boats need the same number of white rods? How were these boats the same? How were they different?

Extending the Activity

Have children repeat the activity, this time using rods to form their own initials. Have them challenge their classmates to estimate, then find the number of white rods that would be needed to cover their initials.

Where's the Mathematics?

In this activity, children estimate and then determine the number of white rods it would take to build their boat. Since a white rod is equivalent to 1 cubic centimeter, children are actually making an estimate about the volume of a free-form shape. Building a boat with 5 to 10 non-white Cuisenaire Rods will result in equivalent boats of 10 to 100 white rods.

This activity will be easier for children who have some familiarity with the length of each rod. Asking children to find the actual number of white rods they would need in two different ways encourages them to use various strategies for counting and to develop ways to check the accuracy of their answers.

To facilitate counting, children may begin to find the actual number of white rods by grouping the rods they used by color. For example, a child might group the like rods in the boat below reasoning that a group of two reds can be covered by 4 whites and a group of three yellows can be covered by 15.

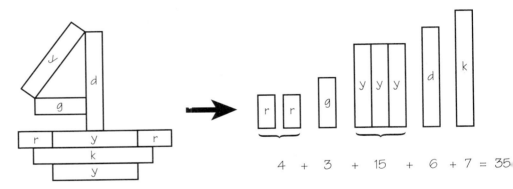

$$4 + 3 + 15 + 6 + 7 = 35$$

Children who have an understanding of base-10 place value might choose to group the rods by tens as shown to the right and then count "10, 20, 29, 35" to find the total.

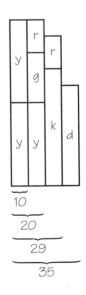

Some children may find it easier to skip count by 5s or 2s or by some other number. They may choose to trade in sets of rods, converting everything to the number they feel most comfortable working with. For example, a child who sees three yellow rods in the boat on the previous page may choose to set aside the 3 yellow rods and trade the remaining rods for an equivalent number of yellow rods then count the 7 resulting yellow rods by 5s: 5, 10, 15, 20, 25, 30, 35.

Children who are proficient with addition may simply record the length of each rod of the boat and find the sum: 5 + 6 + 3 + 2 + 5 + 2 + 7 + 5 = 35.

As they compare their results, children may come to realize that the length of the rods, not the quantity, determines the total number of white rods needed. A boat using fewer rods may require a greater number of white rods to cover it than one using more rods. The boat discussed above uses 8 rods and requires 35 white rods to cover it while the boat shown below uses only 7 rods but requires 41 white rods.

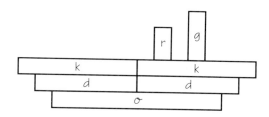

Looking at the number of rods used versus the number of white rods needed to cover them will help children learn that numbers can be used for comparing measurements only if the unit of measurement is consistent. This idea occurs again and again in mathematics. If two children each have five coins, they do not know who has the greater amount of money until the coins have been converted to an identical unit of measurement, say pennies. Likewise, children cannot compare length, capacity, elapsed time, area, or perimeter until they know the unit of measure used for each.

CHALLENGE MATCH

- Equivalence
- Addition
- Game strategies

Getting Ready

What You'll Need

Cuisenaire Rods, 1 set per pair

Overhead Cuisenaire Rods and/or
1-centimeter grid paper transparency
(optional)

Overview

In this game for two players, children take turns matching two-car
Cuisenaire Rod trains to a single rod in an effort to be the last to make
a two-car train. In this activity, children have the opportunity to:

- ◆ find equivalent lengths
- ◆ see that different pairs of addends can have the same sum
- ◆ intuitively use the commutative property of addition
- ◆ develop strategic thinking skills

The Activity

Introducing

- ◆ Show children a yellow rod. Ask them to find two rods that, when
  put end to end to form a train, are as long as the yellow.

- ◆ Establish that there are two different ways to do this.

y	
g	r

y	
p	w

- ◆ Explain that the order of the rods does not make a difference. Show,
  for example, that a green-red train is the same train as a red-green.

y	
g	r

y	
r	g

- ◆ Tell children that they will be playing a game using two-car trains.
  Go over the rules for *Challenge Match* given in *On Their Own*.

On Their Own

Play *Challenge Match!*

Here are the rules.

1. This is a game for 2 players. The object is to pick the Cuisenaire Rod from the pile that cannot be matched by a 2-car train.

2. The first player chooses any rod except for white and challenges the second player to make a matching 2-car train.

   Here are some ways to match an orange challenge rod:

   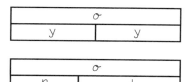
   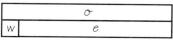

3. When a match is made, the second player takes the challenge rod and the train and picks the next challenge rod.

4. Players take turns picking. Whoever picks the challenge rod that cannot be matched by a 2-car train wins.

• Play 3 games of *Challenge Match.*

• Be ready to talk about good moves and bad moves.

The Bigger Picture

Thinking and Sharing

Invite children to talk about their games and describe some of the thinking they did.

Use prompts such as these to promote class discussion:

♦ How did you decide which rod to give your partner as a challenge?

♦ Were some rods easier to match than others? Explain.

♦ Why was the white rod never used as a challenge rod?

Extending the Activity

1. Have children play the game again, this time using two challenge rods of different colors. The challenge in this game is to find a rod that, when added to the shorter of the two challenge rods equals the length of the longer challenge rod.

2. Have children repeat the game, this time finding three-car trains equal in length to the challenge rod.

Where's the Mathematics?

Challenge Match is a strategy game that has embedded practice in finding sums of 10 or less. When children select the two-car trains to match a challenge rod, they are practicing addition. The child choosing the challenge rod needs to survey the rods remaining in the pile and select a rod that cannot be matched with any two of the others. Both of these tasks require children to think "What plus what will equal this rod?" which provides readiness for subtraction.

At first, children approach the task of picking a challenge rod randomly, choosing any rod from the pile. Some may pick their favorite color or select a rod because there are fewer of that color in the pile. However, as children gain experience playing this game, they begin to see that some choices are better than others, and they will examine the rods left in the pile before deciding which challenge rod to select. The key to winning this game is selecting the one rod for which there are no addends left in the pile. For example, if all of the red rods have been eliminated, matching the light green rod with a two-car train becomes impossible.

A chart of all the possible two-car trains that can match a challenge rod can provide a concrete representation of what many children learn intuitively while playing this game. Helping to develop such a chart will help children see why eliminating all the red or white rods is a good strategy.

Color of Rod	w	r	g	p	y	d	k	n	e	o
Possible 2-car trains	none	w + w	w + r	w + g r + r	w + p r + g	w + y r + p g + g	w + d r + y g + p	w + k r + d g + y p + p	w + n r + k g + d p + y	w + e r + n g + k p + d y + y

A good way to implement the strategy of eliminating red and white rods is to choose short challenge rods. Short challenge rods have few two-car possibilities and require even shorter rods (such as reds and whites) for the matching trains. Conversely, the longer rods have more pairs of addends so the chances of winning when using a long rod as the challenge rod is not as great. As you discuss the possible two-car trains for each challenge rod, you may also find the opportunity to introduce the terms "greater chance" and "less chance" which will become part of the children's vocabulary when they study probability.

The order in which the rods are placed in a train is irrelevant in this activity. As a result, children informally learn the commutative property for addition (white, then purple is the same as purple, then white) as they form their trains.

Playing this game can give children needed practice with their addition facts. Children with weak skills will rely on the trial-and-error method of picking rods whose sum is equivalent to the challenge rod. As children continue to search for matches, however, actually measuring with rods will be necessary less often, and children will begin to develop a knowledge of basic addition facts. Even those children with more developed skills can benefit from the reinforcement of making correct choices and having the rods to manipulate to verify the sum.

COPY AND REPEAT

- • Pattern recognition
- • Counting
- • Comparing

Getting Ready

What You'll Need

Cuisenaire Rods, 1 set per pair

1-centimeter grid paper, page 110

Overhead Cuisenaire Rods and/or
1-Centimeter grid paper transparency
(optional)

Overview

Children use Cuisenaire Rods to form patterns by repeating given designs.
They then determine the number of rods in the patterns. In this activity,
children have the opportunity to:

- ◆ describe a pattern
- ◆ extend a pattern
- ◆ learn that a single core design can be used to create different patterns

The Activity

Here are some ways children might
describe the pattern:

Red, white; red, white; red, white

Tall, short; tall, short; tall, short

Big, little; big, little; big, little

It has three reds and three whites.

It has only two colors.

Every other rod is red.

Introducing

- ◆ Show the following Cuisenaire Rod pattern.
- ◆ Call on volunteers to put down the next two
  rods and explain their choices. Elicit that red and white is the
  correct choice.
- ◆ Ask children to describe the pattern. Make a list of suggestions on
  the chalkboard.
- ◆ Separate the rods as shown. Explain that the class was able to recognize the pattern because each red-and-
  white combination forms a core design
  that was repeated.
- ◆ Repeat the process with a
  pattern such as this one.

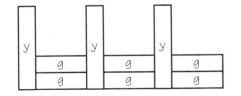

On Their Own

How many Cuisenaire Rods will you need to make a pattern in which a design appears 10 times?

- Work with a partner. Look at the 4 pictures below. In each picture, a basic design of Cuisenaire Rods appears twice. Decide what the pattern is in each picture.

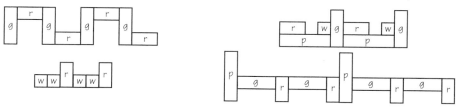

- Choose the basic design in 1 of the pictures. Use it in a Cuisenaire Rod pattern that repeats the design so that it appears a total of 5 times.

- Record your pattern. Count and write down how many rods of each color you used and how many rods you used altogether.

- Imagine continuing your pattern by repeating the design until it appears a total of 10 times. Predict how many rods of each color and how many total rods you would need to do this.

- Now complete the pattern with 10 designs. Count the rods and compare the numbers to your prediction.

- Be ready to talk about what you did and what you found out.

The Bigger Picture

Thinking and Sharing

Create columns by displaying each of the four basic designs across the chalkboard. Then have pairs post their drawings in the appropriate column.

Use prompts like these to promote class discussion:

- Which pattern or patterns took the fewest rods to build? How many of each color rod did you need? How many rods did you need altogether?

- Which pattern or patterns took the most rods to build? How many of each color rod did you need? How many rods did you need altogether?

- What are some ways to predict how many rods you will need before you make a design repeat?

Writing

Have children use Cuisenaire Rods to make up the basic design of a pattern. Ask them to explain how to figure out how many rods of each color and how many rods altogether would be needed to use this design to make a pattern that shows the basic design ten times.

Extending the Activity

1. Have children work with their partners, taking turns creating a pattern and then extending one another's patterns.

2. Have children describe the patterns in other ways: for example, with letters, with claps, or with body motions.

Where's the Mathematics?

This activity gives children the opportunity to identify and extend patterns and then use the patterns to make predictions. Pattern recognition is crucial to accurate counting and reading decoding skills. Until children recognize the existence of patterns and how they can be used, every number from 1 to 100 can appear to them to be unrelated. Once they recognize the recurring pattern of numbers ending in 1, 2, 3, ..., 9, however, they need only the benchmarks of 10, 20, 30, 40, ..., 90 to be able to count from 10 to 100!

As children identify patterns and extend them to involve a given number of repetitions, they are informally introduced to the concept that each pattern has a core (basic) design—the name given to the original set of rods that repeats. Some children may struggle to identify the core design, especially when the design involves the location of the rods as well as the colors. It may help for children to find a way to verbally describe what they see in order to create an auditory, as well as a visual, pattern. For example, the first design might be described, "green, red up, green, red down." In extending patterns, children demonstrate their ability to reproduce the core design that they identify.

Children may use the structure of various patterns to help them calculate the number of rods of each color as well as the total numbers of rods needed for the design. While some children, especially the younger ones, may be unable to find this information without constructing the entire pattern then counting, others may use strategies such as doubling, skip counting, or multiplication. For example, a child might look at the core design below and then skip count to find the number of rods in a pattern that uses the core ten times. The child would reason that since each core design requires 2 light green rods, the number of light green rods in the pattern that uses the core ten times can be found by counting 2, 4, 6, 8, 10, 12, 14, 16, 18, 20. He or she may further notice that each core design also has 2 reds, and conclude that the same number, or 20 reds, is required for the whole design, as well.

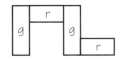

Another child might use doubling to predict the number of rods needed for a pattern showing the core design used ten times. Based on the pattern below that uses the core design five times, the child might reason, "For 5 parts of the pattern, I need 5 reds and 10 whites. There are 10 parts in the whole pattern. So, I need twice as much, or 10 reds and 20 whites." If the child then extends the pattern and counts the rods, he or she can verify the accuracy of the prediction.

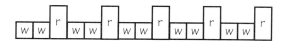

Children also have the opportunity to analyze pattern structure when they talk about how many rods are needed to make the pattern. As they discuss which patterns take the most rods to build, they may be able to generalize that the greater the number of rods in the core design, the greater the number of rods there will be in the completed pattern. A pattern that has only 3 rods in its core design will require 30 rods for the whole structure; whereas a pattern with a core design of 4 rods will require 40 rods. The use of 9 repetitions (10 appearances of the core design) for a pattern will introduce many opportunities for children to practice using the multiples of 10 in their work and their discussions.

Asking children to find the number of each color of rod, as well as the total number of rods needed to make a 10-design pattern, will encourage them to check their work. For example, if they predict that 9 repetitions of the design below will require 50 rods, they can check this number with the prediction that 10 purple, 20 red, and 20 light green rods will be needed. The sum of the parts should equal their prediction for the total number of rods needed.

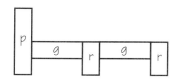

COVER THE GIRAFFE

- Counting
- Area
- Spatial visualization

Getting Ready

What You'll Need

Cuisenaire Rods, 1 rod of each color per child

Cover the Giraffe worksheet, several per child, page 92

Crayons

Overhead Cuisenaire Rods and/or *Cover the Giraffe* transparency (optional)

Overview

Children cover the outline of a giraffe using a specified set of Cuisenaire Rods. They compare their work and try to identify as many different solutions as possible. In this activity, children have the opportunity to:

- ◆ develop spatial reasoning
- ◆ visualize a region as the sum of component parts
- ◆ find multiple solutions

The Activity

Introducing

- ◆ Outline the shape shown on 1-centimeter grid paper. Then copy and distribute it.
- ◆ Challenge children to cover the outline using only 1 white rod, 2 red rods, and 1 light green rod.
- ◆ Establish that several different ways of covering the shape are possible.

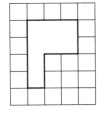

On Their Own

How can you cover the giraffe using just 1 Cuisenaire Rod of each color?

- Work with a partner. Each of you make your own Cuisenaire Rod staircase.

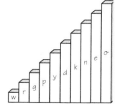

- Now use the rods from your staircase to completely cover a giraffe that looks like this.

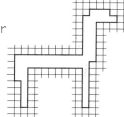

- Compare your work.

- Record both solutions if they are different. Record just 1 of them if they are the same.

- On other worksheets, find more ways to cover the giraffe. Record each way.

- Be ready to talk about how your covered the giraffe.

The Bigger Picture

Thinking and Sharing

Invite children to post their solutions. Lead a discussion about the similarities and differences in the position of the rods

Use prompts such as these to promote class discussion.

- ♦ How many different solutions did the class find?

- ♦ Did finding the first solution make it easier to find more solutions? If so, how?

- ♦ When you began to cover a new giraffe, which rod did you place first? Why?

- ♦ Which rods were hardest to place? Why? Which were easiest? Why?

- ♦ Do you think that there might be even more ways to cover the giraffe? Why do you think so?

Extending the Activity

1. Ask children to use the rods from one of their solutions to figure out how many white rods they would need to cover the giraffe.

2. Have children create their own animal picture or design using one rod of each of the ten colors. Have them trace the outline of their work on 1-centimeter grid paper then challenge others to fill in the outline using only the rods from a staircase.

Where's the Mathematics?

Many children enjoy solving spatial puzzles, such as *Cover the Giraffe*. Some will do these puzzles with speed and ease while others will require more time and many tries. You are likely to find that children who excel at doing this are not necessarily the same ones who do well at computational tasks. Including activities, such as *Cover the Giraffe*, in your classroom can help you meet children's different learning styles.

The initial goal for this activity should be for children to find just one solution. As partners compare their solutions, additional approaches will emerge. This giraffe design has a great deal of flexibility so it lends itself to many solutions. Here are two solutions with quite different rod arrangements—in one case, the orange rod is placed horizontally; and in the other, it is placed vertically.

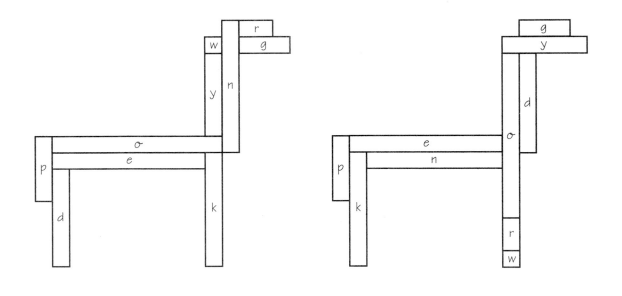

As children study their own and one another's solutions, they may see simple ways to find alternative solutions. For instance, in the right-hand arrangement on the previous page, the light green rod (the top of the head) could be easily switched with the red and white rods and a "new" solution would be found. Another easy switch would be to change the order of the rods in the column containing the orange, red, and white rods. The rods could be placed in different orders, creating "new" solutions. Finding easy switches such as these helps children see a concrete explanation for how one number may have multiple representations.

Children may find that the grid marks outside the outline help them predict which rods will fit inside. They can count the number of grid squares to find the length of the rod that will fit inside the outline. Children frequently find it easier to place the longer rods into the outline first and then move the shorter rods around to fill in the remaining spaces.

This activity provides a chance for children to work with the concept of area on an informal basis. The giraffe has a constant area of 55 square centimeters, but that area may be broken down into smaller areas in scores of different ways. Later, in middle school and in high school, children will use this same idea to break complex areas into smaller shapes that are easier to work with. For example, it is easier to find the area of the complex shape below if it is broken down into a rectangle, a semicircle, and a triangle.

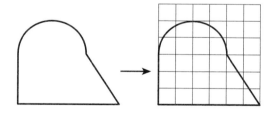

HOW MANY TWO-CAR TRAINS?

• Addition
• Patterns

Getting Ready

What You'll Need

Cuisenaire Rods 1 set per pair

1-centimeter grid paper, page 110

Crayons

Overhead Cuisenaire Rods and/or 1-centimeter grid paper transparency (optional)

Overview

Children select Cuisenaire Rods, then find and record the two-car trains whose lengths match the selected rods. In this activity, children have the opportunity to:

◆ express one rod as a sum of two others

◆ informally use the commutative property

◆ write sentences to model their work

The Activity

Introducing

◆ Ask children to take a black rod and to put two rods on top of it that cover it exactly.

◆ Invite volunteers to share their solutions.

◆ Establish that the solutions shown here are different because the order of the rods differs.

r	y
k	

y	r
k	

On Their Own

> ### How many different 2-car trains can you make for a Cuisenaire Rod?
>
> - Work with a partner. Choose any Cuisenaire Rod other than white.
>
> - Build as many 2-car trains as you can that have the same length as the rod you chose. Here is what the 2-car trains for a purple rod would look like.
>
>
>
> - Record your work. For the purple rod, the recorded work would look like this:
>
> - Repeat this activity for rods of other colors. Record your results for each rod.
>
> - Look for patterns in the number of solutions.
>
>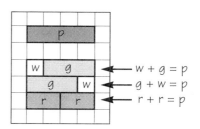

The Bigger Picture

Thinking and Sharing

Ask children for suggestions on how all the data they have collected should be displayed. Then create a table entitled *How Many 2-Car Trains?* and invite volunteers to provide data for each rod.

Use prompts like these to promote class discussion:

- What patterns do you notice?

- Did you have a strategy for finding two-car trains that match the rods? What was it?

- How can you be sure that you found all the possible two-car trains?

- Imagine you had a new rod that was one unit longer than the orange rod. How many two-car trains could you make to match it?

Extending the Activity

1. Have children record their data for each rod in an addition table like this one. Have them look for patterns in their tables.

+	w	r	g	p
w	r	g	p	y
r	g	p	y	
g	p	y		
p	y			

2. Have children investigate the number of three-car trains that can be made for each of the Cuisenaire Rods.

Where's the Mathematics?

This activity provides an opportunity for children to synthesize and review each of the two-addend facts for sums up to 10 and then to take the process one step further by finding the pattern embedded in the answer to "How can you be sure that you found all the possible two-car trains?" Review is provided in three ways: concretely, through the use of the Cuisenaire rods; pictorially, through recording the rod arrangements on grid paper; and symbolically, through writing the number sentence that corresponds to each rod arrangement.

Children who have collected data haphazardly, working with a purple rod first, then a black and then a red rod, may not be able to organize their data so that they can find patterns. Collecting children's work in a class chart that moves in an orderly fashion from smallest to largest can help them see patterns. Creating the chart may help children think about a method of organization the next time they are presented with a situation that involves lots of data.

Some classes may choose to display all the data they have collected. Their chart might begin this way:

How Many 2-Car Trains?

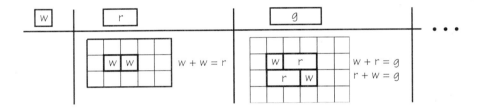

Other classes may choose to display only a summary of their findings. Their chart might look like this:

Color of rod	w	r	g	p	y	d	k	n	e	o
Number of solutions	0	1	2	3	4	5	6	7	8	9

After children have found matches for the first few rods, they may report that once they recorded a train, such as white plus green, they could find another solution by turning the train around and recording green plus white. The only time this does not work is if both cars are the same color; for example, red plus red looks the same even when it is turned around. Some children may notice the pattern that all the odd sums have an even number of two-car train solutions. This is true because all the two-car trains are made up of rods of different lengths and each train can be reordered to form another solution. The even sums, on the other hand, have an odd number of two-car train solutions because every even sum has a train with two cars of the same color that cannot not be turned around to form another solution.

Looking at the number of solutions for each rod, most children see that the number of two-car trains for each rod is one less than the length of the rod. For example, for a light green rod that is 3 units long, 2 trains are possible; whereas, for a purple rod that is 4 units long, 3 trains are possible.

If children were asked to imagine rods longer than the orange, they would find that the pattern continues. For example, an 11-centimeter rod would have 10 matching two-car trains.

JUMPING FROGS

Getting Ready

What You'll Need

Cuisenaire Rods, 1 set per pair

Lily Pad Strips worksheets, 1 per pair, page 93

Crayons

Overhead Cuisenaire Rods and/or Lily Pad Strips transparencies (optional)

Overview

Pretending that a Cuisenaire Rod of a chosen color is a jumping frog, children move the rod along a number line. They then compare the "jumps" taken by several "frogs." In this activity, children have the opportunity to:

◆ investigate the factors of numbers up to and including 20

◆ recognize multiples of the numbers from one to ten

◆ describe patterns

The Activity

Introducing

◆ Display the Lily Pad Strips worksheet.

◆ Hold up a purple rod. Tell children to pretend that the purple rod is a frog. Put the rod on a lily pad strip starting at the zero point. Lead the class in counting the lily pads that the rod covers to determine that the rod is four units long and that it ends at the fourth lily pad.

◆ Demonstrate how to move the rod across the strip to show the frog's jumps, stopping to color every fourth lily pad purple.

• Have children predict how many jumps the frog will need to take to go all the way across the strip.

On Their Own

Make a Cuisenaire Rod "frog" jump! Which lily pads will the frog land on?

- With a partner, choose a rod of any color. Pretend that your rod is a frog that jumps its own length.

- Color the picture of the frog on a lily pad strip the same color as your rod.

- Get your frog ready to jump. Make it jump onto the lily pad strip starting at O. Color the lily pad at the end of the jump the same color as your frog. Here's an example.

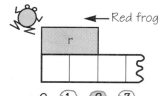

- Jump again! Start this jump where the first jump ended. Color the lily pad at the end of each jump. Here's an example:

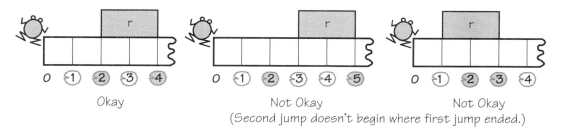

Okay   Not Okay   Not Okay

(Second jump doesn't begin where first jump ended.)

- Make your frog keep jumping until it has jumped all the way across the strip, coloring the lily pads at the end of each jump.

- Now choose a rod of a different color. Make this frog jump its own length along a new lily pad strip. Color to show the jumps. Do the same for different colored rods.

- Cut your lily pad strips apart. Compare them. Look for patterns.

- Be ready to talk about what you find out.

The Bigger Picture

Thinking and Sharing

Write the colors, from *white* to *orange*, as column headings across the chalkboard. Call on pairs to post their lily pad strips in the appropriate columns.

Use prompts like these to promote class discussion:

- What do you notice about the posted lily pad strips?
- How are the strips the same? How are they different?
- Which frogs' jumps could you predict? Why?
- At which lily pads did the _____ (name a color) frog land?

Extending the Activity

1. Have children do the activity again, this time using a longer strip made by taping two or more strips of centimeter grid paper end to end.

Where's the Mathematics?

Jumping Frogs provides a playful setting for exploring the concepts of factors and multiples as readiness for the formal study of multiplication and division. As the frogs jump from zero to twenty, the notion of multiplication as repeated addition is established. Between studying their individual lily pad strips and assembling the data on a completed chart such as the one shown below, children will be able to identify a variety of patterns.

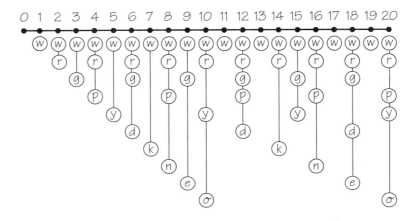

The first pattern many children note is the link between the lily pads and the ordinal numbers. They will point out that the light green frogs stopped on every third lily pad, the purple frogs on every fourth pad, the yellow frogs on every fifth, and so forth. This occurs, of course, because the frogs are repeatedly making jumps of the same length. Children may also point out the inverse relationship that the longer the jump, the fewer it took to get across the lily pad strip or, conversely, the shorter the jump, the more it took to get across. Some of the frogs, namely the light green, dark green, black, brown, and blue ones, never reach 20 in an exact number of jumps.

2. Have children write addition and subtraction number sentences for each of the jumps shown on their lily pad strips.

Children will also note certain color patterns, such as that every lily pad the purple frogs stopped on was visited by the red frogs, too. Some will take this a step further and note that the purple frogs stopped on every other lily pad that the red frogs visited. Children who study the chart closely will see that if both the red and light green frogs stop on a lily pad, then they can predict that a dark green frog will land there, too. These observations are preparing children to recognize common multiples, important in the addition and the subtraction of fractions with unlike denominators. For example, the first step in adding $\frac{1}{2}$ and $\frac{1}{3}$ is to find that the common denominator is 6 which is similar to recognizing that whenever a red and light green frog stop on a lily pad, dark green frog will stop there as well.

Some children will note that certain lily pads are very popular stopping places indeed! Lily pads #12 and #20, for instance, are each visited by 5 different frogs, while lily pads #8 and #16 have 4 visitors apiece. Other lily pads, such as 1, 11, 13, 17, and 19 are visited only by the white frogs that stopped on every lily pad. The notion that some numbers, such as 8, 12, 16, and 20, are very rich in factors while other numbers have very few factors will be revisited for the purposes of dividing whole numbers and simplifying fractions. Fractions that have these factor-rich numerators and denominators are more likely to be fractions that can be simplified while fractions composed of 11, 13, or 17 in the numerator or denominator probably cannot be further simplified.

LOAD THE TRUCKS!

- Addition
- Chance
- Game Strategies

Getting Ready

What You'll Need

Cuisenaire Rods, 1 set per pair

Truck Spinner 1, 1 per pair, page 94

Truck Spinner 2, 1 per pair, page 95

Load the Trucks! worksheet, 1 per child, page 96

Crayons (optional)

Overhead Cuisenaire Rods and/or *Load the Trucks!* worksheet transparency (optional)

Overview

In this game for two players, children take turns spinning one of two spinners in order to collect enough Cuisenaire Rods to fill four trucks, each of which carries a 10-centimeter-long "load." In this activity, children have the opportunity to:

- ◆ create models of sums of 10
- ◆ learn about the effect of "chance"
- ◆ use strategic thinking

The Activity

Introducing

- ◆ Display an orange rod. Make a rod train as long as the orange rod such as the one shown.

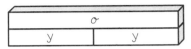

- ◆ Ask children to build a different train that is as long as the orange.
- ◆ As volunteers describe their trains, build them in view of the class to confirm that each matches the orange rod.
- ◆ Tell children that they will be playing a game called *Load the Trucks!* Explain that the load on each truck should be as long as an orange rod.
- ◆ Play part of a demonstration game with a volunteer before children begin *On Their Own.*

On Their Own

Play *Load the Trucks!*

Here are the rules.

1. This is a game for 2 players. The object is to be the first to load 4 trucks with Cuisenaire Rods.

2. Players take turns spinning either of these spinners.

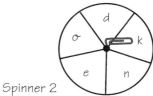

Spinner 1   Spinner 2

3. After each spin, the player loads a matching rod onto the back of a truck that looks like this.

Load Here →

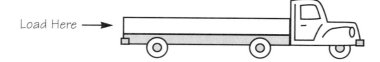

4. Each truck can hold a load equal to 10 white rods. Once a rod is loaded on a truck, it may not be moved to another truck. If a player spins a rod that does not fit on any truck, then that player loses a turn.

5. Players keep on spinning and loading rods on the trucks until the trucks are fully loaded.

6. The first player to load all 4 trucks wins the game.

• Unload your trucks! Now play the game 2 more times.

• Be ready to talk about how you loaded your trucks.

The Bigger Picture

Thinking and Sharing

Invite children to talk about their games and describe some of the thinking they did.

Use prompts such as these to promote class discussion:

◆ After you spun for a rod, how did you decide where to load it?

◆ Did you ever have trouble finding a place to load a rod? Explain.

◆ How did you decide which spinner to use on a turn?

◆ Did you ever load any rods that you wanted to take back? Explain.

◆ Did your strategy change as the trucks came close to being fully loaded? If so, how?

◆ Did you learn any strategies from your first game that helped you when you played again? Explain.

Writing and Drawing

Have children pretend that they have just loaded a black rod onto a truck. Direct them to tell which other rods could be added to complete the load. Then have children draw the truck and show the black rod and the other rod or rods that make up their load.

Where's the Mathematics?

This activity develops children's spatial sense and number sense as they load each truck with Cuisenaire Rods that have a total length of 10 centimeters. Facility with working with numbers whose sum is ten underlies many mental math strategies. Providing opportunities to make sums of ten will set the stage for children's understanding of base-10 place value and of the trading that is often needed in working with arithmetic algorithms.

At first, some children will use trial and error deciding where to place the rod they spun. For example, they may take a purple rod and try to squeeze it onto a truck already loaded with a black or brown rod. As they gain experience, their ability to judge the length of a rod and the amount of available space on a truck will improve. They will begin to realize that purple may only be loaded onto trucks containing rods equal to or shorter than a dark green.

Children will see examples of the commutative property of addition when, for example, they compare a truck loaded with yellow, white, and purple rods with a truck loaded with white, yellow, and then purple. If children write number sentences for their trucks, they will recognize that the order of the numbers does not matter when performing addition; that is, 4 + 2 has the same sum as 2 + 4. This can cut the work of learning the addition facts in half! Children also develop familiarity with the idea that the operation of addition can involve more than two numbers.

Extending the Activity

Have children play the game again. This time, have them record the rods that make up each of their loads by writing a number sentence. For example, for a load consisting of three light green rods and one white rod, a child would write "3g + 1w = 10w."

When children discuss how they decided to load each truck, they may point out a strategy for losing fewer turns. For example, if a child had a truck loaded with a black rod, a truck loaded with a purple rod, and two empty trucks and then spun light green, it would be wise to put the light green next to the black rod. This move would complete one truckload while leaving room on the purple truck for any rod from white to dark green. Applying this strategy requires critical thinking, especially at the point in the game when few trucks have been completely loaded and children must look at several trucks before they decide which truck is the best one to load next.

Having a choice about which spinner to use can help children develop some strategies about how to use probability to work to their advantage. At first, children may use the spinners with little forethought. They might choose the spinner with their favorite color on it, alternate using one spinner then the other spinner, or they might select the same spinner their partner chose. As they gain experience, many children will report that they learned to use Spinner 2 in order to spin the longer rods at the beginning of the game and then moved to Spinner 1 in order to spin the shorter rods towards the end of the game. In the middle of the game, children might report looking at the spinners and thinking, for example, "I could use two of the rods on this spinner or four of the rods that are on the other spinner so I would be better off choosing the one that has the four rods that would be useful."

MAKE A MATCH!

- Spatial visualization
- Congruence
- Following directions

Getting Ready

What You'll Need

Cuisenaire Rods, 1 set per pair

Books or heavyweight folders to use as barriers

1-centimeter grid paper, 1 sheet per child, page 110

Overhead Cuisenaire Rods and/or 1-centimeter grid paper transparency (optional)

Overview

Children take turns making secret shapes from Cuisenaire Rods. They describe their shapes to their partners, who then try to make shapes that match the descriptions. In this activity, children have the opportunity to:

- ◆ identify attributes of Cuisenaire Rod shapes
- ◆ communicate specific information
- ◆ strengthen listening and visualizing skills

The Activity

Introducing

- ◆ Build this Cuisenaire Rod shape and keep it hidden.

- ◆ Tell children that you have made a shape which you will show to them later. Explain that they are to make a matching shape according to the directions you will give them.

- ◆ Give step-by-step directions for building the shape. Include the color of the rods, their orientation, and "looks like . . ." statements.

- ◆ When everyone is ready, reveal your shape and have children compare theirs to yours.

- ◆ Ask children to tell which words you used in your directions that helped them to imagine what the shape—or part of the shape—looked like.

On Their Own

How can you describe a Cuisenaire Rod shape you have made so that your partner can make it, too?

- Work with a partner. Decide who will be the Shape Builder and who will be the Matchmaker. Set up a barrier so that neither of you can see the other's workspace.

- When you are the Shape Builder:
    - Secretly choose from 3 to 10 Cuisenaire Rods.
    - Make a secret shape with the rods.
    - Give clues about the shape to help a partner make a matching shape.

- When you are the Matchmaker:
    - Listen carefully to the clues.
    - Try to make a matching shape.

- When the Matchmaker is ready, take the barrier away. Check to see if you have matching shapes.

- Do the activity 3 more times. Take turns being the Shape Builder and the Matchmaker. Leave your last pair of shapes in place.

- Be ready to talk about making secret shapes and matching shapes.

The Bigger Picture

Thinking and Sharing

Ask a pair to display the last two shapes they made. The Shape Builder should try to recall the directions he or she gave. The Matchmaker should try to explain what he or she did in response to each direction. Invite the class to comment on the directions and the shapes.

Use prompts such as these to promote class discussion:

- Was it easier to be the Shape Builder or the Matchmaker? Why?
- What words did you use to describe the different rods?
- What words helped you know where to put rods or how to line them up?
- When you were a Matchmaker, what kind of directions did you think helped the most?
- What tips would you give to another Shape Builder? to another Matchmaker?

Drawing

Tell children to draw the shape they liked best. It may be one that they designed as a Shape Builder or one that they built from directions as a Matchmaker.

Extending the Activity

1. Have partners repeat the activity. This time, however, instead of the Shape Builder giving clues, the Matchmaker poses questions to help him or her build the secret shapes. For example, a Matchmaker may ask, "Which rods are in your shape?" or "Should I put the light green rod next to the purple?"

Teacher Talk

Where's the Mathematics?

Spatial vocabulary plays an important role in learning mathematics, yet children sometimes lack experience in both using and interpreting this vocabulary. As you listen to what the Shape Builders say during this activity, you will notice the terms that need introduction or clarification. Children will probably identify the various rods they use by color, but placement of these rods may involve either the correct terms or informal equivalents for concepts such as *above, below, right, left, perpendicular, horizontal, vertical, distance,* and *angle.*

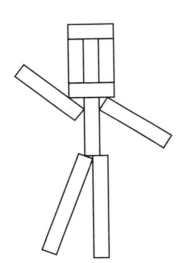

Many children start with overall descriptions that are not easy to follow. They may say, "I made a person," which is not very helpful unless they also describe which rods to use and how the various parts of the body are positioned. Even if children say something like, "The head is made from four light greens, the body from a purple, the arms from yellows, and the legs from black," results might be as different as those shown at left.

A good description will probably include words that indicate direction, such as *under, over, on top of, right, left, bottom, top,* and words that indicate shape, such as *rectangle, square,* or *triangle.* Young children may use body language, as well. For instance, instead of saying "right," a child might say, "Put two rods on this side," and wave his or her right hand in the air to underscore what is meant by "this side." If children are sitting across from one another rather than side by side, this use of body language may actually cause listeners to put the two rods on the left, because the listeners followed what they saw, which was a hand waving on their left side.

The opportunity to use mathematical language in context is crucial in the construction of mathematical understanding. Mathematical terms such as

2. Have pairs work together as "Shape Builders." Then have them either write a set of directions or record a set of directions on audio tape. Have them exchange their directions with another pair and work together as "Matchmakers," trying to build the other pair's shape.

---

ten, third, between, and *next to* provide children with the means to give a more precise description of the structure. It is a good idea to keep a running list of mathematical terms on a chart for all to see and refer to. This list should be compiled as the terms emerge in context and become part of the dialogue. In this way, the word is connected to an experience, helping to make discussion of the term meaningful. In addition, pictures or diagrams drawn next to some terms on the list can provide a good visual reference.

In comparing two shapes, children have an opportunity to deepen their understanding of congruence. Children may need to scrutinize their shapes carefully to determine whether or not they are identical, and, if not, how they differ. The two shapes may be congruent, but, because of their different orientations, children may not think they are identical.

The task of comparing shapes provides immediate feedback for the partners on how well they were able to communicate with one another. Children should be encouraged to try to figure out which descriptions may have been misinterpreted and to discuss better ways of explaining or describing those particular attributes of the shapes.

Children should recognize that the goal of the Shape Builder is not to try to trick the Matchmaker, but rather to provide useful descriptions that will enable the Matchmaker to build an exact replica of the Shape Builder's structure. This is not a competitive activity. The importance of the skills brought to the task by both partners—describing, listening, visualizing, and questioning—become more and more evident as children repeat the activity and take turns at the two roles.

This activity may be difficult for some children since it relies both on the vocabulary of the Shape Builder and his or her ability to organize directions in a sequence that makes sense and on the listening and interpreting skills of the Matchmaker. Because these skills are in a constant state of development, you can use this activity over and over again to assess growth in both vocabulary and interpreting skills. You can also use it after you have modeled vocabulary to see what progress has been made.

MIRROR MONSTER

- Spatial visualization
- Symmetry
- Congruence
- Transformational geometry

Getting Ready

What You'll Need

Cuisenaire Rods, 1 set per pair

1-centimeter grid paper, several sheets per pair, page 110

Mirror, 1 per pair

Overhead Cuisenaire Rods and/or 1-centimeter grid paper transparency (optional)

Overview

Children build a Cuisenaire Rod arrangement on one side of a line drawn on a grid. Then they build the mirrored image of the arrangement in an effort to make a symmetrical figure, a "mirror monster." In this activity, children have the opportunity to:

◆ develop an understanding of symmetry

◆ practice left-right differentiation

◆ describe a shape's location with respect to the location of its reflected image

The Activity

To demonstrate how to use a mirror to check for symmetry, hold it along the chalkboard line perpendicular to the board. Point out that if the reflection children see when they peek into the mirror shows the matching part of the outline (the part on the other side of the mirror) then they can be sure that the line is a line of symmetry.

Introducing

◆ Draw a vertical line on the chalkboard. Hold a small toy against the board so that just one corner of it touches the line. Trace around the toy on the board.

◆ Still holding the toy in this position, demonstrate how to flip it across the line. Trace around it in its new position.

◆ Ask children what they notice about the two outlines.

◆ Repeat the activity, this time starting with a horizontal line.

◆ Elicit that each pair of outlines is separated by *a line of symmetry* and that a pair of outlines together show *symmetry*. Explain that children can check for symmetry by using a mirror to prove that the outline on one side of the line is a *mirrored image* of the outline on the other side.

On Their Own

> ## How can you make a Cuisenaire Rod "mirror monster"?
>
> - With a partner, choose 4 or more Cuisenaire Rods. You will use these rods to make part of your monster.
>
> - Fold a piece of grid paper in half along 1 of the lines on the paper. Unfold the paper and draw a line along the fold.
>
> - Make the first part of your monster by putting your rods on the grid on 1 side of the line so they touch each other. Make sure that at least 1 rod touches the line.
>
> - Pretend the line is a mirror that goes through your mirror monster's middle! Get more of the same rods. Put them on the other side of the line to show how a mirror would reflect the first part of your monster. You may use a real mirror to check your work.
>
> - Leave your completed monster where your classmates can see it.

The Bigger Picture

Thinking and Sharing

Allow pairs to walk around the room to observe one another's mirror monsters. Encourage them to look at each monster carefully, checking to see that the part on one side of the line of symmetry is a reflection of the part on the other side.

Use prompts such as these to promote class discussion:

- Which side of your monster did you build first?

- How did you go about building the part on the other side of the line?

- How are the two parts of your monster alike? How are they different?

- Do any other monsters look exactly like yours? Do any look just a little like yours? Which ones?

- Were there any monsters that looked a lot like yours but that were made from different rods? Which rods were they?

- Was it easier to put down some rods on the other side of the line than others? Explain.

Drawing

Distribute 1-centimeter grid paper, each with a heavy rule drawn down the middle, to match the ways children folded their papers. Tell children to think of the rule as the line that goes down the middle of their monster. Have them use crayons to record the rods they used to make the first part of their monster. Then have them record the mirrored image of that part on the other side of the line of symmetry.

You may wish to show children how to check their recordings by folding along the fold line and observing whether the two sides of the recording fit over each other exactly.

Extending the Activity

Invite children to repeat the activity, this time folding their papers to get a different line of symmetry from the one used before. That is, if they previously folded their papers from side to side to get a vertical line of symmetry, have them now fold their papers from top to bottom to get a horizontal line of symmetry and *vice versa*.

Teacher Talk

Where's the Mathematics?

As children use Cuisenaire Rods to make mirrored images in this activity, they are working with the concept of reflective, or line, symmetry. Opportunities to use vocabulary, such as *vertical, horizontal, right, left, square,* and *rectangle* will arise naturally when children discuss their designs. You may also wish to make references to length as children work on their designs. You may say, for example, "This red rod is 2 centimeters long and you placed it 5 centimeters to the left of the line of symmetry. How far to the left do you have to place its mirrored rod?"

Children will develop various strategies for making the mirrored images. Many will depend solely on intuition, placing the mirrored rods and moving them around until the design "feels" in balance. Some may choose to hold a Cuisenaire Rod in the same orientation as the original rod and then flip it over the line of symmetry and drop it into place. Others will think of the mirrored image as being the opposite, or a backwards version, of the original image. They may count to help them put the rods into place. If the first purple rod is located 3 squares away on the right-hand side of a vertical line of symmetry, they will run a finger along the horizontal line that the purple rod is resting on and then place the mirrored purple rod 3 squares away on the left-hand side of the line of symmetry. Pointing as they count helps children keep the mirrored rod in place horizontally as well as vertically.

Some common errors children may make in trying to show the mirrored image as shown below are (1) not flipping the design, (2) positioning a piece the wrong distance from the fold line, and (3) positioning a mirrored piece above or below the original piece.

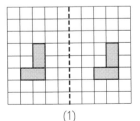 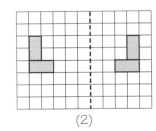 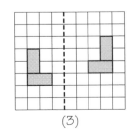

(1) (2) (3)

As children become more comfortable making their own symmetrical designs, they may notice that there is only one place in which each matching rod can be positioned to make a mirrored image.

Every Cuisenaire Rod has two lines of symmetry.

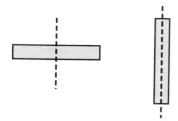

Children may take advantage of these lines of symmetry and let some of their rods "straddle" the line of symmetry. For example, if they used a dark green rod, they might place it so that 3 centimeters of the rod are on the left side of the line of symmetry and 3 centimeters are on the right side of the line of symmetry. Or they may place the dark green rod so that the rod's line of symmetry that runs the length of the rod is placed on the line of symmetry for the design. The two "mirror monsters" shown here incorporate this idea of having the rods straddle the line of symmetry.

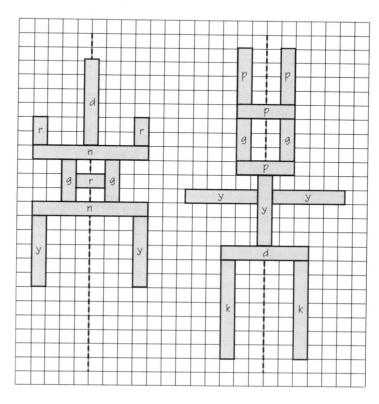

Some children will experience more difficulty if they try to build a mirrored image along a horizontal line of symmetry than if they try to build it along a vertical line of symmetry. This is probably because more objects, both naturally occurring and manufactured, exhibit vertical lines of symmetry, and so the eye is more familiar with making left-right shifts than making up-and-down shifts across a line of symmetry.

MYSTERY TRAINS

• Deductive Reasoning
• Spatial reasoning

Getting Ready

What You'll Need

Cuisenaire Rods, 1 set per pair

Mystery Trains Clue Cards 1 and 2, 1 set per pair, pages 97-98

1-centimeter grid paper, page 110

Crayons

Overhead Cuisenaire Rods and/or 1-centimeter grid paper transparency (optional)

Overview

Children follow a set of clues to make one or more Cuisenaire Rod trains. In this activity, children have the opportunity to:

◆ reason deductively

◆ work with problems that may have multiple solutions

◆ improve spatial reasoning

The Activity

Introducing

◆ Tell children that you are thinking of a mystery train made of Cuisenaire Rods and that you will give them clues about the train, one at a time, so that they can build it.

◆ Give children the following clues. After each clue, allow time for children to make adjustments to their trains.

> *My train is as long as a dark green rod.*
> *My train has three rods.*
> *Each rod is a different color.*

◆ Invite volunteers to show their solutions and explain their reasoning.

◆ Repeat the activity changing the first clue to *My train is as long as a blue rod.*

◆ Elicit that there are several solutions to this new set of clues.

On Their Own

> **Can you build the Cuisenaire Rod Mystery Train described on a clue card?**
>
> - Work with a partner. Choose a Mystery Train clue card.
>
> - Use the clues to build the train with your Cuisenaire Rods.
>
> - When you think you have built the mystery train, read the clues again and check your work. Make changes if you need to. Many clue cards have more than 1 solution.
>
> - Try to build a different train for your clue card.
>
> - Record all the trains you built. Write the number of the clue card next to each train.
>
> - Select another clue card and repeat the activity.
>
> - Be ready to talk about how you built each mystery train.

The Bigger Picture

Thinking and Sharing

Write *Mystery Train #1, Mystery Train #2,* and so on across the chalkboard. Have pairs of children post solutions under the appropriate headings.

Use prompts such as these to promote class discussion:

- Which mystery trains were the easiest to build? Which were hard? Why?

- How did you go about building a mystery train?

- Did you change the pattern as you worked? Why or why not?

- What can you learn from this clue (read one clue aloud)? What do you still need to find out?

- Why was it important to read the clues after you had built a mystery train?

Writing

Have pairs of children create their own *Mystery Trains* by using three or four Cuisenaire rods to create a train and then writing clues about how to make it. Groups can trade clues and try to build one another's *Mystery Trains*.

Extending the Activity

1. Have children write a number sentence for each train. For example, for a red-red-dark green train, children would write 2 + 2 + 6 = 10.

Where's the Mathematics?

This activity provides rich opportunities for children to use logical thinking to work out a set of clues and try to determine if more than one solution is possible. If you choose to have children write number sentences to describe each train, children will see that a number may have multiple representations.

Most children read the clues to learn the limitations on the rods they may use and then employ a "guess-and-check" strategy to figure out the final train configuration. Some children stop after they have found one solution and may need to be encouraged to look for additional solutions.

The solutions for each Mystery Train are given below.

Mystery Train #1	Mystery Train #2	Mystery Train #3	Mystery Train #4
5 r	5 g	2r + d	w + d
10 w	15 w	r + g + y	r + d
		r + 2p	g + d
		r + n	

Mystery Train #5	Mystery Train #6	Mystery Train #7	Mystery Train #8
2g + r + w	2w + g + p	2r + 2p	p + d + n
2r + w + p	2w + k	3w + 3g	
2w + r + y	2r + w + p		
2w + g + p	2g + w + r		
	2p + w		

Deductive reasoning is a process of reaching a conclusion from one or more statements. Children get practice in deductive reasoning by analyzing clues, eliminating possibilities, and organizing information. Focusing on one clue and asking children what they can and cannot conclude helps them learn not to jump to conclusions or read more into the clue than is there. Hearing

2. For clue cards with multiple solutions, have children create additional clues that will eliminate all but one solution.

3. Have children solve mystery cards that you have created for other manipulatives such as Pattern Blocks, Tangrams, or Color Tiles.

the clue, "Each car is shorter than a purple rod," allows children to conclude that the train must be composed of white, red, and/or light green rods. From this clue alone, children cannot conclude anything about how many cars are on the train or how long the train is. If the next clue reads, "All the cars are the same color," children can conclude that only one of these colors has been used, but they cannot conclude which one. Adding the final clue, "The train is as long as an orange rod," finally limits the mystery train either to a train of 5 red rods or a train of 10 white rods. Children frequently forget to go back and combine the new knowledge they learned with previous clues that they have heard. These clue cards will give them practice in combining bits of information to make one complete whole.

Children are likely to have more difficulty with clues involving negations such as, "There are no yellow cars," than they will have with the positive clues, such as, "The shortest car is red." Statements that are negations are a fact of life and helping children to translate negative clues into positive clues will help them solve a variety of problems. Some of the clues include comparison phrases, such as "shorter than a purple rod," or "more than 3 cars," which may be misinterpreted by children. For example, they may omit the comparison and interpret "shorter than a purple rod" as meaning that the train includes a purple rod, or they may limit the rod choices to light green and overlook the fact that white and red rods are also possibilities.

The order of the cars on the train is not addressed in these clues. Some children will represent one of the solutions to Mystery Train #3 as red, then brown while other children will record it as brown, then red. Seeing these two representations exposes children to the commutative property of addition which states that the order of the addends does not matter; that is, 2 + 8 is the same as 8 + 2.

Looking back over one's work is an important part of being a good problem solver, particularly when logic is involved. One faulty conclusion can cause a whole series of errors in later logic. Hearing the clues again and looking at their work critically can help children identify errors or open up the possibility of finding additional solutions.

ROD LOTTO

- Spatial visualization
- Comparing
- Congruence

Getting Ready

What You'll Need

Cuisenaire Rods, 1 set per group

Small paper bags, 1 per group

Rod Lotto game boards, 1 sheet per group, page 99

Crayons (optional)

Overhead Cuisenaire Rods and/or *Rod Lotto* game boards transparency (optional)

Overview

In this game for two to four players, children take turns picking Cuisenaire Rods from a bag and placing matching rods on their game boards in an effort to be the first to completely cover their game board. In this activity, children have the opportunity to:

- ◆ identify the ten Cuisenaire Rod colors
- ◆ become familiar with the lengths of the rods
- ◆ observe the different ways in which Cuisenaire Rods can be combined into a rectangular configuration

The Activity

Introducing

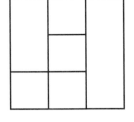

- ◆ Prepare copies of an actual-size outline of this configuration of Cuisenaire Rods. Distribute the copies.
- ◆ Demonstrate how to match a rod to one part of the outline and to cover that part with the rod. Have children do the same.
- ◆ Invite volunteers to continue matching rods to the outline on display until it is completely covered. Have children complete their own outlines.
- ◆ Together with the class, count the number of pieces needed to cover the square outline. Be sure that children understand that six rods— one red, four white, and one light green—were needed to cover it completely.

On Their Own

Play *Rod Lotto!*

Here are the rules.

1. This is a game for 2 to 4 players. The object is to be the first to cover 1 of these game boards.

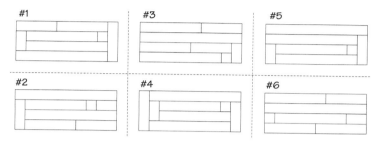

2. Each group needs a bag filled with 1 of each color of Cuisenaire Rod. Each player takes 1 game board. Players decide who will be first to pick a rod.

3. The first player picks a Cuisenaire Rod from the bag without looking, shows it to the group, then returns it to the bag. All players try to match 1 rod of that color to a space on their game board.

4. Players take turns picking a rod and replacing it. Each time, players check their game boards to see if they need a rod of that color.

5. The first player to completely fill a game board is the winner.

- Play several games of Rod Lotto.
- Be ready to tell about your games.

The Bigger Picture

Thinking and Sharing

Invite children to talk about their games and describe some of the thinking they did.

Use prompts such as these to promote class discussion:

- When it was your turn to pick, did being able to feel the rods help you? If so, how?
- If you needed more than one rod of a color for your game board, did it matter where you put the rod the first time it was named?
- Is there a way to be good at winning this game? Why or why not?
- Do you think that all players have a fair chance of winning this game? Explain.

Drawing

Have children record how their boards looked when the last game they played ended.

Extending the Activity

1. Have children play *Rod Lotto* again, this time calling out the numbers from one to ten, instead of naming colors, to identify the rods.

Teacher Talk

Where's the Mathematics?

On the surface, *Rod Lotto* looks as if it is a very simple game, but do not be deceived. Playing it gives children an opportunity to increase their ability to make visual estimates of length. Most children do not have difficulty looking at their board and recognizing when they need the longest rod, orange, or the shortest rod, white. For many children however, the ability to recognize the lengths of rods between these two extremes is not so well developed. For example, they may have difficulty determining whether the outline on the board requires a yellow rod or a dark green rod because these two rods are only 1 centimeter apart in length.

In actuality, the game is fair. Each board requires 8 rods to cover a total of 40 square centimeters. The colors have been distributed fairly—all the boards have at least one white and one red rod, 5 of the boards have at least one purple rod, and each of the other 7 colors is distributed on 4 of the 6 boards.

For children who are visual learners, repeating this game just a few times markedly increases their ability to distinguish whether they need a yellow or a dark green rod. Some children also report using visual clues on the board to help them. For example, consider this board:

#3

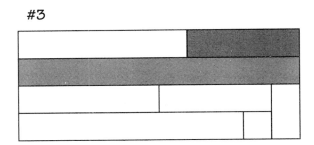

Children familiar with Cuisenaire Rods may report that they know that a dark green rod plus a purple rod is equivalent in length to an orange rod, and so they know that they need a dark green rod for the upper left-hand corner. Other children may report a variation on this idea saying that they realize that each *Rod Lotto* board is 10 centimeters wide and since the purple is 4 centimeters, they used subtraction to help them figure out that

2. Suggest that children play *Rod Lotto* again, but this time, instead of having them pick rods from a bag, provide them with one of the sets of cards needed for the *Rod Squeeze* lesson. Have players take turns picking a card from the set and reading each card aloud for all players to react to.

---

10 – 4 is 6, so they need the dark green rod that corresponds to a length of 6.

When the boards are filled in, children can scan across the board looking at different length configurations whose total is 10 centimeters. For example, consider this completed board:

 #5

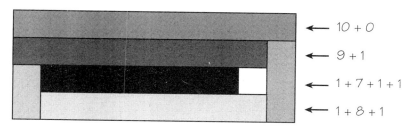

← 10 + 0
← 9 + 1
← 1 + 7 + 1 + 1
← 1 + 8 + 1

In this case, the top row has a single orange (10) rod. Below this, 10 appears as a blue (9) rod plus 1 centimeter of a light green rod. The next row shows 10 as 1 centimeter of a red rod plus a black (7) rod plus a white (1) plus 1 centimeter of a light green. The bottom row shows still another way to find a sum of 10.

When asked to decide whether this game is fair to everyone, children have many opinions. Some children do not realize that every Lotto board requires 8 rods. Some mistakenly think that if their board has several short rods clustered together, such as in the lower right-hand corner of board #3 which requires a red, a white, and a purple rod, that they need more rods than do some other players. Likewise, some children think that boards #2 and #5 that have long blue and orange rods on them require fewer rods.

Some children suggest that having boards #1, #3, or #6 makes it harder to win because each of these boards requires two rods of one color while the other boards only require one of each color. Others respond to this and say that needing two of one color on a board makes it easier to win because when that color is called the second time, only one person benefits and everyone else "loses a turn."

ROD SQUEEZE

- Counting
- Addition
- Subtraction
- Spatial visualization
- Game strategies

Getting Ready

What You'll Need

Cuisenaire Rods, 1 set per pair

Rod Squeeze game board 1,
1 per child, page 102

Rod Squeeze cards set 1, 1 per pair,
page 100

Rod Squeeze game board 2,
1 per child, page 103 (optional)

Rod Squeeze cards set 2, 1 per pair,
page 101 (optional)

Overhead Cuisenaire Rods and/or
Rod Squeeze game boards 1 and 2
transparencies (optional)

Overview

In this game for two players, children solve Cuisenaire Rod sentences, then place the solution rods on their game boards in an effort to leave fewer squares uncovered than their opponent. In this activity, children have the opportunity to:

- find sums and differences of rods in terms of their lengths
- associate a rod with a numerical value
- develop strategic thinking skills

The Activity

Be sure children are familiar with the Cuisenaire Rod notation. If necessary, review the letter designations for the rods (see Introductory material).

Introducing

- Write a rod sentence, such as $g + p = \square$, on the chalkboard.
- Invite a volunteer to complete the sentence, using rods to show light green and purple equal black, or $g + p = k$.
- Repeat the process with the following sentences.

$$p - r = \square$$
$$\square + k = o$$
$$n - \square = y$$
$$d + \square = e$$

- Tell children that they will use sentences like these to play a game in which they will fit Cuisenaire Rods on a game board.
- Go over the game rules given in *On Their Own*.

On Their Own

Play *Rod Squeeze!*

Here are the rules.

1. This is a game for 2 players. The object of the game is to place Cuisenaire Rods on a game board so that all the squares are covered.

2. Each player takes a game board that looks like this.

3. Players place the *Rod Squeeze Cards Set 1* face down between them. They take turns picking a card, reading it aloud, then placing it in a discard pile.

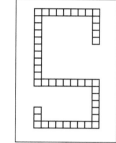

4. Each time a card is read, players agree on the rod that is needed, and each places that rod somewhere on his or her game board.

5. Once a rod is placed, a player cannot move it.

6. If there is no room on the game board to place the required rod, the player waits for the next card to be read.

7. The winner is the player who, after all the cards have been drawn, has the least number of squares uncovered.

- Play *Rod Squeeze* at least 4 more times using the same game board.
- Be ready to talk about good moves and bad moves.

The Bigger Picture

Thinking and Sharing

Invite children to talk about their games and describe some of the thinking they did.

Use prompts such as these to promote class discussion.

- Which rods were the easiest to fit on the game board? Which were the hardest to fit? Why do you think this is so?
- What did you notice as you played the game?
- Did you ever make a move you wished you could take back? Explain.
- What helped you decide where to place a rod?
- Was it important to plan ahead? If so, why? Give an example.

Extending the Activity

1. Have children play the game again, but this time using *Rod Squeeze* game board 2. Ask them to compare what happens with what happened when they played on game board 1.

2. Have children play the game again, using either game board, but this time with *Rod Squeeze Cards Set 2*.

Teacher Talk

Where's the Mathematics?

Rod Squeeze embeds concrete practice with addition, subtraction, and counting using Cuisenaire Rods within the context of a strategy game that also involves an element of luck (or chance). Children associate rods with numerical values based on the white rod being equal to 1 unit. As children play, they count the game board squares over and over again to see, for example, if placing the yellow rod still leaves 9 squares for the blue rod. The key to winning the game is the ability to plan ahead and leave room for the longer rods that are apt to turn up on later game cards.

As the children's experience with playing the game increases, they will make three discoveries that influence their strategies. The first discovery is that there is a one-to-one correspondence between the ten different color rods and the ten cards in the clue set. Since each card has a sentence that is made true with a different colored rod, over the course of the game, all ten rods will be possible choices. Children who realize this will think ahead and try to avoid boxing themselves in.

The second discovery that children will make is that there are a limited number of playing positions for the longer rods. For example, on the S-shaped game board, the orange rod will fit in one of only two positions on the long vertical side. If a player places a shorter rod (other than white) vertically on this side, the orange rod can no longer be played, and at least 2 squares will remain uncovered at the end of the game.

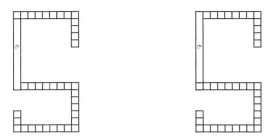

Likewise, the blue rod can be played only along one of the three horizontal bars of the S-shape, but its placement may depend on where the orange rod was placed. Once the orange and blue rods have been placed, the number

3. Suggest that children play *Super Rod Squeeze* by playing on both game boards at once and using both sets of cards mixed together. The winner of this game is the one who puts down the last rod on the second board to be completely filled.

of positions left for the brown and black rods becomes limited. And so, to minimize the number of uncovered squares left at the end of the game, a player must think ahead and leave openings for the orange and blue rods.

The third discovery is that every game will have certain rods that cannot be played. The game board has 47 squares and the set of 10 rods requires 55 squares so even with the most careful playing, some rods will be left over. The element of luck now comes into play. The order in which the clue cards are drawn will have an impact on which of those rods is left.

With the "right" luck and careful planning, all of the squares can be covered. There are many ways to accomplish this. Two possibilities are illustrated below.

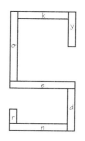   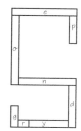

Leftover rods: purple, light green, white   Leftover rods: black, white

When children reflect on their games, their response to "Which rods were easiest (or hardest) to place?" will depend on their viewpoint. Some think small rods are easier to place because there are so many possibilities for their placement. Others think the small rods are harder to place because if those rods are not positioned carefully, they can make it impossible to place the longer rods later in the game.

As children gain more experience with this game, more ties will occur. At this point, it becomes time to challenge them with a different game board and let them see if the old strategies they have learned will translate to a new setting.

ROD TOYS

- Counting
- Comparing
- Spatial visualization
- Money

Getting Ready

What You'll Need

Cuisenaire Rods, 1 set per pair

Tape

Overhead Cuisenaire Rods (optional)

Overview

Children use Cuisenaire Rods to design "toys." Then they find the cost of their toys based on an assigned value for the white rod. In this activity, children have the opportunity to:

- ◆ compare and combine numerical quantities
- ◆ build addition skills
- ◆ work with money concepts

The Activity

Introducing

- ◆ Outline the letter shape shown on 1-centimeter grid paper.
- ◆ Invite volunteers to cover the *E* with Cuisenaire Rods of their choice. Then ask them to count to find how many white rods they would use for the letter.
- ◆ Tell children to suppose that each white rod costs a penny. Ask how much the *E* would cost if they could "buy" it.
- ◆ Elicit that the letter costs (20¢). Have volunteers show why this is true.

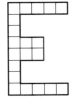

74 *the Super Source™* ◆ Cuisenaire® Rods ◆ Grades K-2   ©1996 Cuisenaire Company of America, Inc.

On Their Own

> ### How can you use Cuisenaire Rods to make a toy for a classroom toy store?
>
> - Work with a partner. Each of you take some Cuisenaire Rods to make a toy that you think other children would like to play with.
>
> - When you are pleased with your toy, have your partner help you tape it together.
>
> - Record your toy. Trace around it. Write letters on the tracing to show the colors of the rods. Here's an example: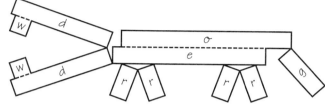
>
> - Pretend that a white rod costs 1¢. Based on this, figure out how much your toy should cost.
>
> - Write the cost of your toy below the tracing.

The Bigger Picture

Thinking and Sharing

Write the heading *Toy Store* at the top of the chalkboard. Invite children to post their tracings across the board according to the cost of their toys, from least to most costly.

Use prompts such as these to promote class discussion:

- What do you notice?
- After you made your toy, how did you go about finding its cost?
- Can anyone suggest another way to find the cost of the same toy? Explain.
- Do any toys that look the same cost different amounts? Which ones? Why?
- Do any toys that look different cost exactly the same amount? Which ones? Why? Which rods were used for each?

Writing and Drawing

Have children make a list of the rods they could use to make a 50¢ toy. Then have them draw the toy.

Extending the Activity

1. Challenge children to find the cost of their toys if the white rod costs 2¢.

2. Ask children to make their initials with rods, then find the cost of their initials if the white rod costs 1¢.

Where's the Mathematics?

Listening to the strategies that children use to figure out the total cost of their toys gives you an opportunity to assess the sophistication of their computation skills. For example, children may approach the problem of finding the cost of this "toy" in several ways.

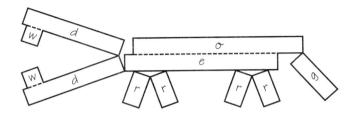

One child might find the cost of each of the eleven rods, listing them, one below the other, so that they can add them. Another child might group the rods using repeated addition or multiplication to find the subtotal for each group and then finding the grand total for all the groups. Their thinking might lead to a list that looks like this:

2 whites @ 1¢	=	2¢
2 dark greens @ 6¢	=	12¢
1 orange	=	10¢
1 blue	=	9¢
4 reds @ 2¢	=	8¢
1 light green	=	+ 3¢
Total		44¢

Breaking the list down into smaller groups of like-colored rods has the advantage of having only six numbers to add to find the grand total. Adding this shorter list of numbers may prevent computational errors. A few children, who feel very comfortable working with money, might choose to make trains of the rods of lengths equivalent to quarters, dimes, or nickels.

o	10¢
e · w	10¢
d · r · r	10¢
d · r · r	10¢
g · w	+ 4¢
Total	44¢

Another child might "walk" a white rod along the entire design, counting 1, 2, 3, ..., 44¢. This method might lead to an error if the child forgets whether or not a rod has been counted already or if the child miscounts and compounds the error by continuing to count on from the wrong number.

Some children may need to place actual coins next to each rod in their design and then find the value of the coins as the final step in finding the cost of their toy.

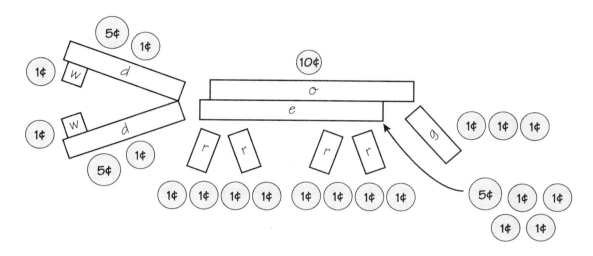

Using the question, "Can anyone suggest another way to find the cost of the same toy?" challenges children to focus on the process rather than on the answer, since the answer is already known. It is important for children to hear and see that there are many approaches to solving a problem. This helps them develop better mental math skills and increase their repertoire of problem-solving strategies.

Children are apt to design very different-looking toys using completely different collections of rods, yet they may end up with some toys that cost the same amount of money. The notion that two different designs can have the same value (area), but look different, is an important mathematical concept.

SIDES OF A TRIANGLE

• Spatial visualization
• Addition
• Counting

Getting Ready

What You'll Need

Cuisenaire Rods, 2 sets per pair

Challenge Cards 1-3, 1 set per pair, pages 104-106

Orange Triangles workmat, 10 per pair, page 107

Overhead Cuisenaire Rods and/or Orange Triangles workmat transparency (optional)

Overview

Children search for combinations of Cuisenaire Rods that will cover the sides of a triangle exactly. In this activity, children have the opportunity to:

◆ represent sums of 10

◆ look for different arrangements of rods

◆ collect and analyze data

The Activity

Introducing

◆ Prepare and display a square rod outline whose sides match the yellow rod.

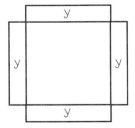

◆ Invite a volunteer to cover the sides of the square with rods.

◆ Call on other children to cover the sides using a different set of rods.

◆ Establish that the least number of rods needed to cover the sides is four yellow ones, but that there exist other solutions that use more than four rods.

On Their Own

How many different ways can you use your Cuisenaire Rods to cover the sides of an orange triangle outline?

- Work with a partner. Choose a *Challenge Card* and follow the directions for covering a triangle outline that looks like this:

- When you think you have found all the solutions, select another *Challenge Card* and follow its directions.

- Be ready to talk about your solutions for each challenge you do.

The Bigger Picture

Thinking and Sharing

Write the Challenge Card numbers 1, 2, and 3 across the top of the chalkboard. Invite pairs of children to come forward and post a recording that shows a solution to one of the challenge cards under the appropriate heading. Call additional pairs of children forward to post different solutions.

Use prompts such as these to promote class discussion:

- ◆ Did you find more than one solution for each of the three challenges? Explain.

- ◆ Once you put one rod on a side, how were you able to predict the rest of the rods that would fit on the side?

- ◆ What patterns did you notice? Describe them.

- ◆ Which challenge did you find the hardest? the easiest? Why?

- ◆ How are these two solutions (cite any two) the same? How are they different?

Writing and Drawing

Have children explain with words or drawings how their solutions to a challenge differed from their partner's.

Extending the Activity

1. Have children repeat this activity using a triangle outline made from a tracing of three blue rods.

2. Have children write number sentences to match the sides of their triangles. For example:

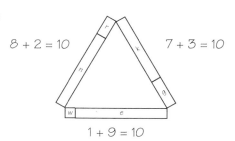

$8 + 2 = 10$ $7 + 3 = 10$

$1 + 9 = 10$

Where's the Mathematics?

This activity combines an opportunity to use spatial reasoning with some practice finding numbers whose sum is 10. This prepares children to understand that a number can be represented in many ways. For example, if the white rod equals 1, then children can see that 10 may be represented as 9 + 1, 8 + 2, 4 + 5 + 1, 2 + 2 + 2 + 2 + 2, and so forth.

Challenge 1 has multiple answers. Here are several possibilities along with numerical representations of the sides:

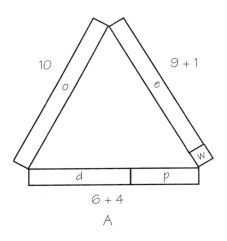

A

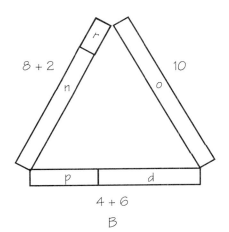

B

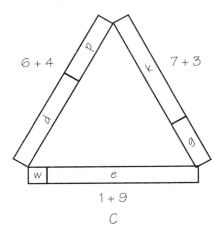

C

Children will find many variations on these triangles. For example, they might take the e + w side from Triangle A, substitute it for the r + n side in Triangle B, and have another solution. Children might also think that the following solutions are different when, in fact, they are not.

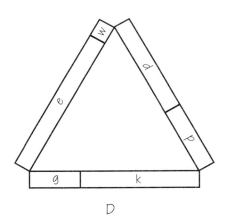

D

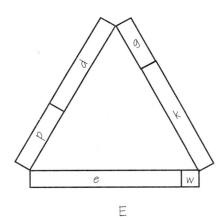

E

Triangle D, is simply a rotation of Triangle C, whereas Triangle E is a rearrangement of the rods on each side of Triangle C. Recognizing the similarities in the sides of the triangles reinforces the commutative property of addition which states that the order of the addends does not affect the sum; that is, 7 + 3 has the same sum as 3 + 7.

Challenge 2 with its limited number of rods has only one basic solution. Children will find many variations on this solution by interchanging the rods on each side or by moving the rods from one side to another.

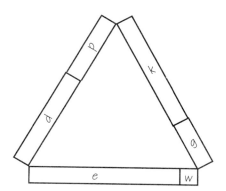

Challenge 3 has four solutions. The triangle may be covered with 30 white rods, 15 red rods, 6 yellow rods, or 3 orange rods. This challenge sets the stage for the children to think about the factors of 10: 1, 2, 5, and 10.

THIRTEEN IS OUT!

- Spatial visualization
- Addition
- Counting
- Game strategies

Getting Ready

What You'll Need

Cuisenaire Rods, 1 set per pair

Thirteen Is Out! game board, 1 per pair, page 108

Overhead Cuisenaire Rods and/or *Thirteen Is Out!* game board transparency (optional)

Overview

In this game for two players, children take turns deciding whether to put a white, red, or light green Cuisenaire Rod on a game board in an effort to avoid being the one to cover the number thirteen. In this activity, children have the opportunity to:

- ◆ work with sums whose addends are 1, 2, and/or 3
- ◆ anticipate an opponent's moves
- ◆ develop strategic thinking skills

The Activity

Introducing

- ◆ Tell children that they are going to play a game called *Thirteen Is Out!* Distribute the game boards.
- ◆ Go over the game rules given in *On Their Own.*
- ◆ Invite a volunteer to play a demonstration game with you.
- ◆ After the first move, point out that the player started from number 1 on the game board.
- ◆ After the second move, point out that the two rods make a train. Tell children each new rod must touch the end of the last rod.

On Their Own

Play *Thirteen Is Out!*

Here are the rules.

1. This is a game for 2 players. The object is to force your partner to cover the 13 on a game board that looks like this.

2. Players put some white, red, and light green rods in a pile. They decide who will go first.

3. The first player takes a rod from the pile and puts it on the game board starting at 1.

4. The second player takes another rod and uses it to make a train with the rod already on the game board.

5. Players take turns making the train longer. No player may skip a turn or leave a space between the rods. Before each of their moves, players think about which color rod their partner might put down next.

6. When a player puts down a rod that covers the 13, the other player wins the game.

- Play *Thirteen Is Out!* 3 more times. Take turns going first.

- Be ready to talk about good moves and bad moves.

The Bigger Picture

Thinking and Sharing

Invite children to talk about their games and describe some of the thinking they did.

Use prompts such as these to promote class discussion:

- ◆ On your turn, how did you decide which rod to put down?
- ◆ Do you think that going first or going second has anything to do with who wins?
- ◆ Did you know whether you would win or lose even before a game ended? How did you know?
- ◆ Is there a way to be sure of winning this game? Explain.

Writing

Ask children to tell how they decided whether to put a white, red, or light green rod on the game board when it was their turn to put down a rod.

Extending the Activity

1. Have children play the game again, this time trying to be the one who covers the number thirteen.

Where's the Mathematics?

The rules in *Thirteen is Out!* are easy for children to understand. The game moves quickly, so children have ample time to play many games, formulate strategies, and test them. After some experience playing the game, children may discover a winning strategy which they can put into practice even if they are unable to put it into words. Children who are unable to articulate their strategies will still be engaging in a considerable amount of problem solving, thus gaining reinforcement of simple addition facts as they cover their game boards.

Most children will, at first, try a relatively random strategy, explaining, for example, that to win, "You should play any rod until you get above 8 and then play very carefully." Others may test strategies that sound systematic, but that are not based on an analysis of the situation. Copying what the other player does or thinking that the first person to play is always the winner (or the loser) are examples of this type of strategy. Some children will develop a strategy, test it once successfully, and be convinced that it will always work. These children need to be encouraged to see that one success is not always enough to judge the validity of a strategy. What is most important in this activity is developing the ability to reason out a situation and think ahead to predict the consequences of a particular action.

If children claim that they can't think of any strategy, suggest that they set their rods aside in the order in which they played them. This enables them to study the pattern which might help them formulate a strategy. One child can place the rods he or she played above the game board while the other child can place his or her rods below the game board. This will help them see the evidence and recall what they have been doing.

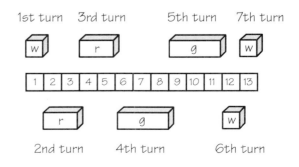

2. Help children double their game board number lines and mark them to 26 in order to play *Twenty-six Is Out!* Allow children to choose three different colors of rods with which to play this game. Lead them to compare the outcome of this game with the outcomes of their games of *Thirteen Is Out!*

After playing a number of times, children will begin to notice that they have lost if they are left with 9 as the first exposed number.

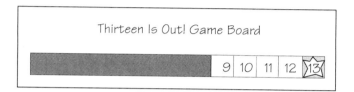

In this situation, whatever they do, their opponent can put down a rod that covers 12, leaving only 13 for them to cover. For example, if they put down a light green, their opponent can put down a white, which would force them to cover the 13 on their next turn. The same sort of reasoning leads children to see that they will lose if 5 is the first exposed number or if 1 is the first exposed number. The winning strategy is to go second and then be sure to put down rods so that 5, 9, and 13 are the first exposed numbers. In other words, the player who goes second must make sure that 4, 8, and 12 are the last numbers covered on his or her turn. This strategy works because the white, red, and light green rods can always be combined in pairs to form a train that covers 4 squares on the game board.

First player	Second player	Squares covered
white	light green	4
red	red	4
light green	white	4

The game board of 13 squares can be thought of as 3 "chunks" of 4 centimeters plus 1 centimeter more. The second player uses the constant sum of 4 to wind up covering the twelfth square and forcing the first player to cover the thirteenth.

WHAT'S IN A SCOOP?

Getting Ready

What You'll Need

Cuisenaire Rods, 2-4 sets per group

Small paper cups (or other small "scoops"), 1 per child

What's In a Scoop? worksheet, 1 per child, page 109

1-centimeter grid paper, page 110

Overhead Cuisenaire Rods and/or 1-centimeter grid paper transparency (optional)

Overview

Children take scoopfuls of Cuisenaire Rods. Then they find different ways to determine the number of white rods that could replace the rods in their scoop. In this activity, children have the opportunity to:

- ◆ count and relate numerical quantities
- ◆ improve logical reasoning skills

The Activity

Introducing

- ◆ Display a green rod and ask children how many white rods could be traded for it.
- ◆ Now display a rod of a different color and ask the same question.
- ◆ Continue in this way until you feel that children understand that each rod can be traded for a corresponding number of white rods.

On Their Own

> **If you traded a scoop of Cuisenaire Rods for white rods, how many white rods would you have?**
>
> - Work in a group. Each of you needs a scoopful of rods and a worksheet that looks like this.
>
> - Empty your scoop in front of you. Record how many of each color rod you have.
>
> - Think about ways to find the number of white rods that you could trade for all your rods.
>
> - Now figure out and record the number of white rods. Tell each other your results and how you found them.
>
> - Leave your rods in place. Be ready to tell the class how you found the number of white rods for your scoopful.

My scoopful had the following rods:

_____ white	_____ dark green
_____ red	_____ black
_____ light green	_____ brown
_____ purple	_____ blue
_____ yellow	_____ orange

I can trade my scoopful for _____ white rods.

Here is how I figured it out:

The Bigger Picture

Thinking and Sharing

Make a chalkboard list of the numbers of white rods that children found for their scoopfuls. Then, ask children to describe how they found their actual counts. As each child speaks, have the class gather around the speaker's rods.

Use prompts such as these to promote class discussion:

- How many white rods can you trade for a ———— (name a color) rod?

- What is one way to find the number of white rods needed for your scoopful? What is another way?

- Who in your group needed the most white rods to equal his or her scoopful? Who needed the fewest?

- Did any of you find that you could trade your rods for the same number of white rods as someone else? If so, how are your scoopfuls alike? How are they different?

Writing

Have children describe how they would find the number of white rods that could be traded for a scoopful consisting of 1 brown rod, 2 purple rods, 1 red rod, and 1 orange rod.

Extending the Activity

Challenge children to choose rods to make up 10 different "scoopfuls" that could be traded for 30 white rods (or another appropriate number of white rods). For each scoopful, have pairs of children compare and verify one another's findings.

Where's the Mathematics?

Listening to the strategies that children use to find the total number of white rods that would replace their scoopful will give you a chance to assess the sophistication of their skills in counting and computing. For example, children may approach the problem of finding the number of white rods in a scoop that contains 2 browns, 2 yellows, 2 reds, 1 dark green, and 1 light green rod in several ways.

Initially, children may try to solve this problem by lining up white rods against each of the rods in their scoop. Since this method is time consuming and the reserve of white rods is likely to be exhausted before the answer is found, children are apt to search for new ways to solve the problem. They might make note of the number of white rods that replace the first rod and then re-use the white rods to measure the length of the next rod. Continuing in this manner they will collect eight numbers to add. Adding such a long list may be daunting for young children so it might be appropriate to suggest the use of a calculator.

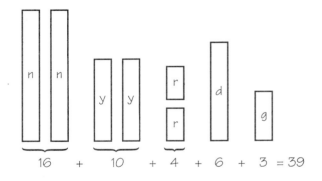

Other children might group the rods together and use repeated addition or multiplication to find the subtotal for each group of rods and then find the grand total of all the rods. By forming groups of like-colored rods, children shorten the list of numbers they need to add and reduce their chances of making computational errors. Their work might look like this.

Children who are experienced with the concept of place value might choose to group the rods so that they can count by 10s as shown below left. This grouping might lead a child to mentally move part of a rod to make even more groups of 10, allowing that child to skip count by 10s and then add the extras on at the end: 10, 20, 30, 39.

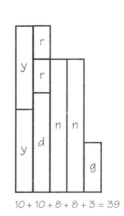

$$10 + 10 + 8 + 8 + 3 = 39$$

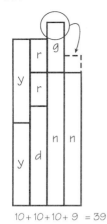

$$10 + 10 + 10 + 9 = 39$$

Another example of using place value is to make a train using all the rods and then compare it to another train composed totally of orange rods. This shows that the rod collection is just one white rod shy of 4 orange rods, so it has a length of 40 − 1, or 39, white rods.

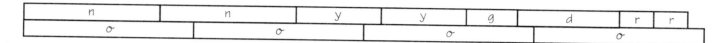

When two or more children find that their rod collections could be traded for the same number of white rods, placing the rod collections side by side, as shown, may lead to some interesting comparisons. For example, children might look at the rods they have in common and comment, "We both have 2 yellows, 2 reds, and a light green. Your dark green and brown is as long as my orange and purple which leaves my black and white which is as long as your brown."

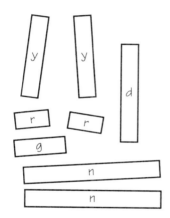
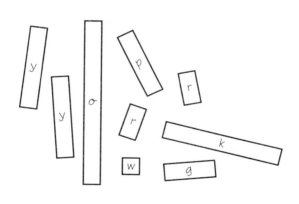

Alternatively, children might stretch each of their rod collections to form a train and compare the lengths of the two trains.

n		n		d	y		y		g	r	r

y		p	y	w	o			k		r	r	g

Making such comparisons helps children learn that one number may have many different representations. Comparing also shows children that changing the grouping of a set of numbers does not affect the final sum—a notion formally known as the associative property of addition. For example, adding 2 + 5 and then 3 yields the same sum as adding 5 + 3, then 2, or (2 + 5) + 3 = 2 + (5 + 3).

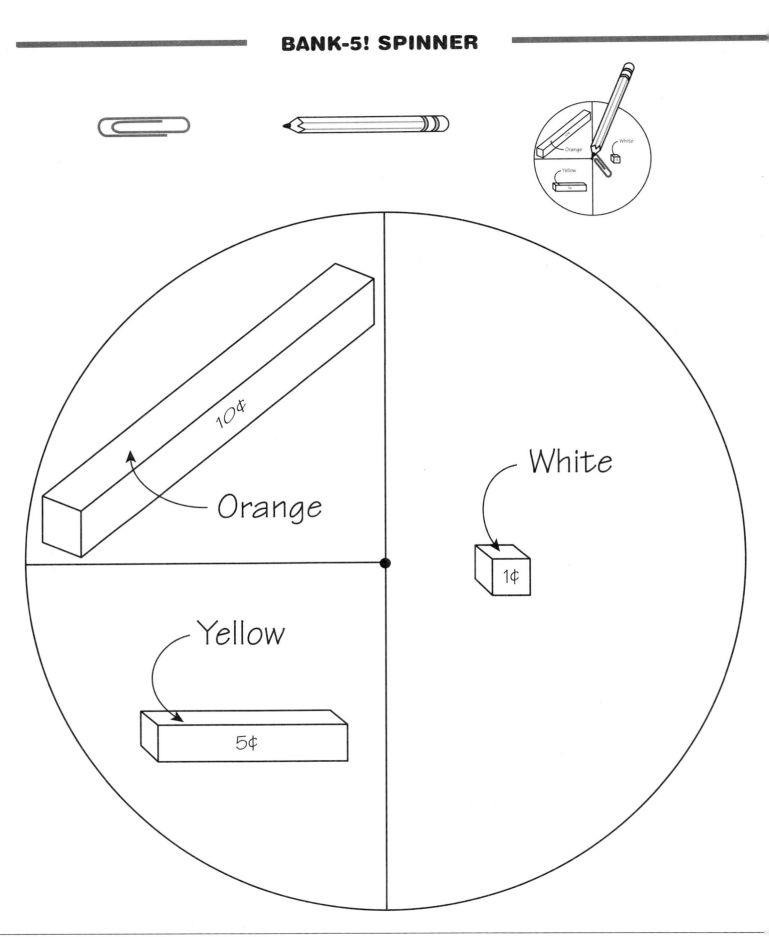

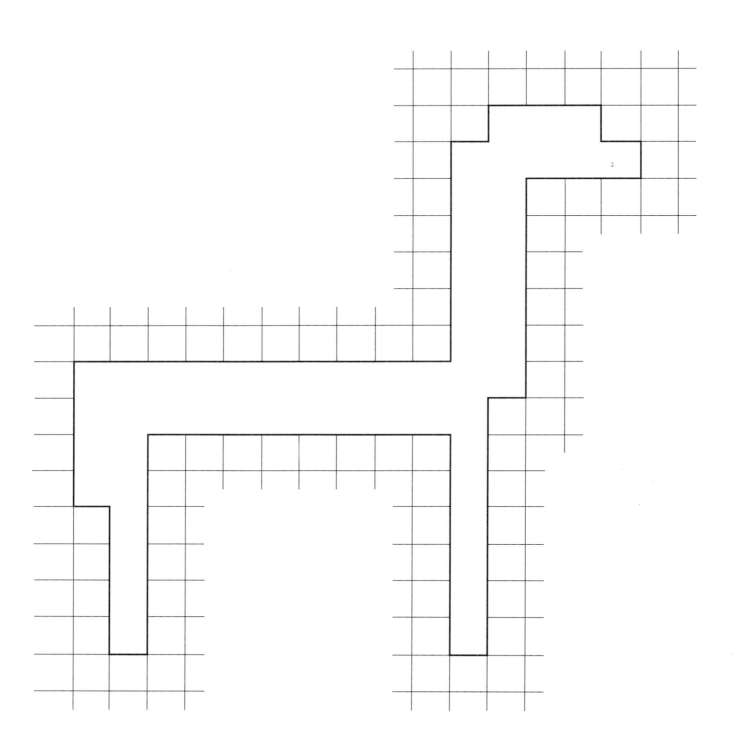

LILY PAD STRIPS

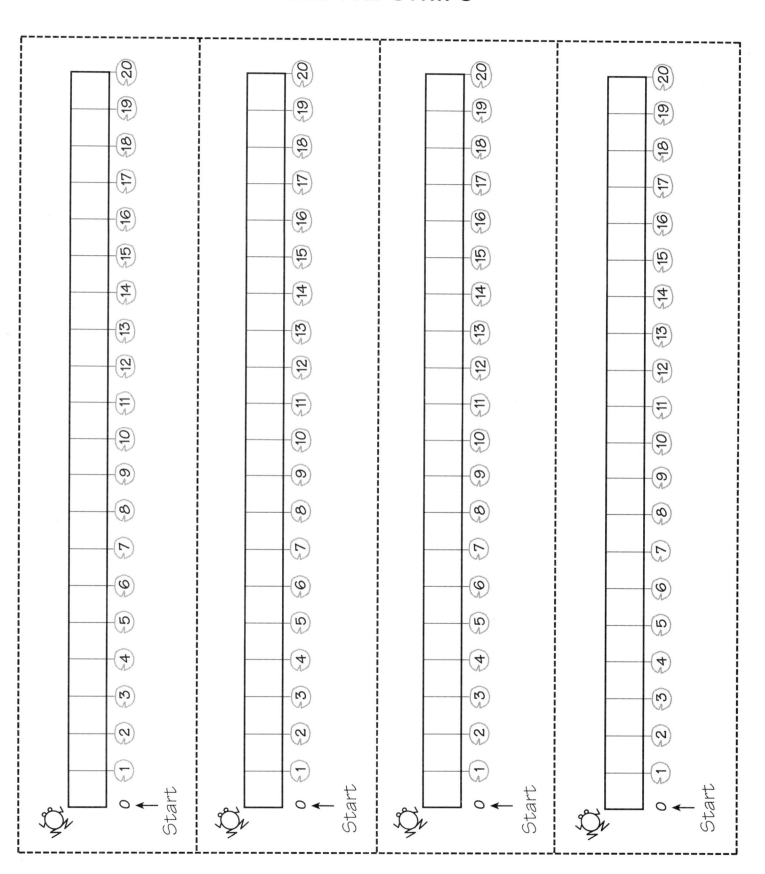

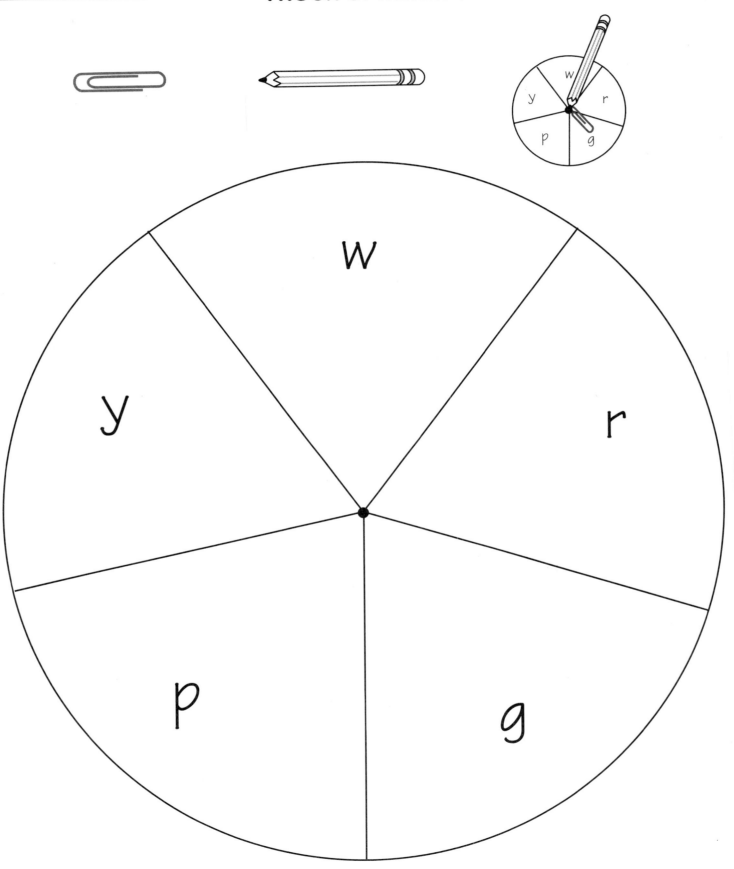

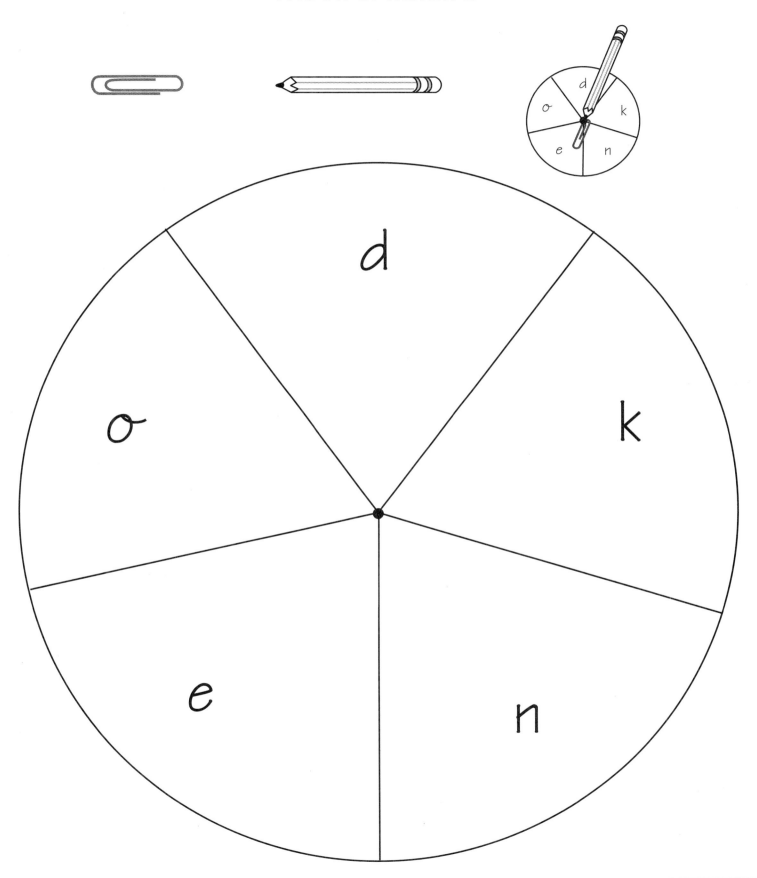

LOAD THE TRUCKS!

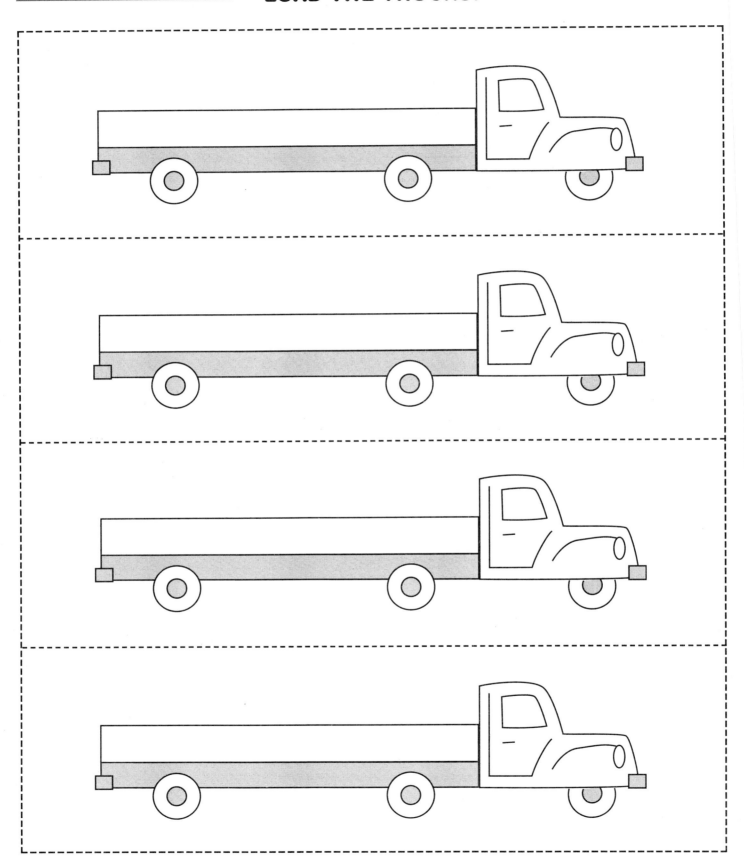

Mystery Train #1

1. Each car is shorter than a purple rod.

2. All the cars are the same color.

3. The train is as long as an orange rod.

Is there more than one solution?

Mystery Train #2

1. The train is as long as a black and a brown rod.

2. All the cars are the same color.

3. There are more than 3 cars.

Is there more than one solution?

Mystery Train #3

1. This train is as long as an orange rod.

2. The shortest car is red.

3. There are fewer than 4 cars.

Is there more than one solution?

Mystery Train #4

1. The train has a dark green rod.

2. This train has only 2 cars.

3. The train is at least as long as a black rod but no longer than a blue rod.

Is there more than one solution?

Mystery Train #5

1. The train is as long as a blue rod.

2. Exactly 2 of the rods are the same color.

3. The train has 4 cars.

Is there more than one solution?

Mystery Train #6

1. This train is as long as a blue rod.

2. Exactly 2 of the rods are the same color.

3. No yellow rods are used.

Is there more than one solution?

Mystery Train #7

1. This train is as long as a blue and a light green rod.

2. Half the cars are one color. Half the cars are another color.

3. There are no yellow cars.

Is there more than one solution?

Mystery Train #8

1. This train has 3 cars.

2. The longest car is brown.

3. Each car is 1 red rod longer than the last car.

Is there more than one solution?

ROD LOTTO GAME BOARDS

#4

#5

#6

#1

#2

#3

ROD SQUEEZE CARDS - SET 1

r + g = ☐	o − r = ☐
w + p + w = ☐	d − y = ☐
g + g + g = ☐	e − y = ☐
p − r = ☐	r + r + r + p = ☐
d − g = ☐	g + p = ☐

$$o - \square = r$$

$$\square + p = n$$

$$\square + w = o$$

$$\square - w = d$$

$$\square + \square = p$$

$$e - \square = d$$

$$\square - g = k$$

$$\square + n = e$$

$$n - \square = r$$

$$\square + \square = o$$

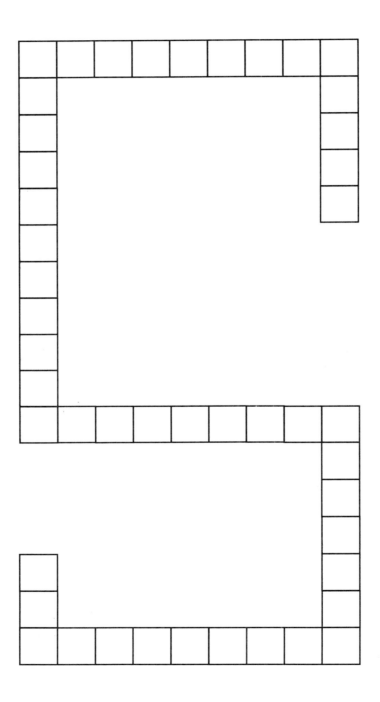

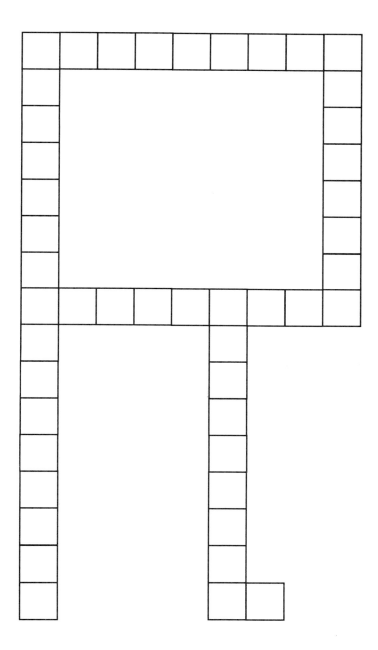

- Make a staircase of Cuisenaire Rods like this one.

- Use an Orange Triangles workmat.

- Cover the 3 sides of a triangle using some of the rods in your staircase.

- Record your solution on the workmat. Do this by coloring the sides to match the colors of the rods used or by writing down the color names to show how you placed the rods.

- Write the challenge card number on your workmat recording.

- Look for more solutions. Record each one on a different workmat.

How many different solutions can you find?

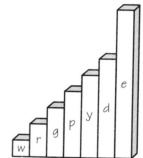

- Make a staircase of Cuisenaire Rods like this one.

- Use an Orange Triangles workmat.

- Cover the 3 sides of a triangle using all of the rods in your staircase.

- Record your solution on the workmat. Do this by coloring the sides to match the colors of the rods used or by writing down the color names to show how you placed the rods.

- Write the challenge card number on your workmat recording.

- Look for more solutions. Record each one on a different workmat.

How many different solutions can you find?

- Use a whole set of Cuisenaire Rods and an Orange Triangles workmat.

- Cover the 3 sides of a triangle using rods that are all the same color.

- Record your solution on the workmat. Do this by coloring the sides to match the colors of the rods used or by writing down the color names to show how you placed the rods.

- Write the challenge card number on your workmat recording.

- Look for more solutions. Record each one on a different workmat.

How many different solutions can you find?

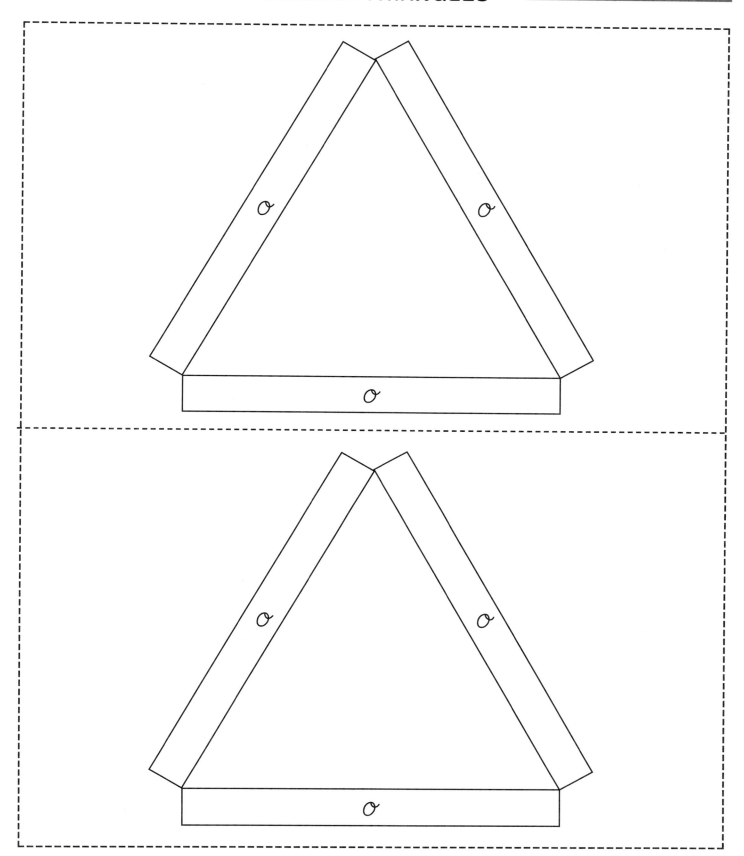

THIRTEEN IS OUT!
GAME BOARD

| 1 | 2 | 3 | 4 | 5 | 6 | 7 | 8 | 9 | 10 | 11 | 12 | ☆13 |

TWENTY-SIX IS OUT!
GAME BOARD

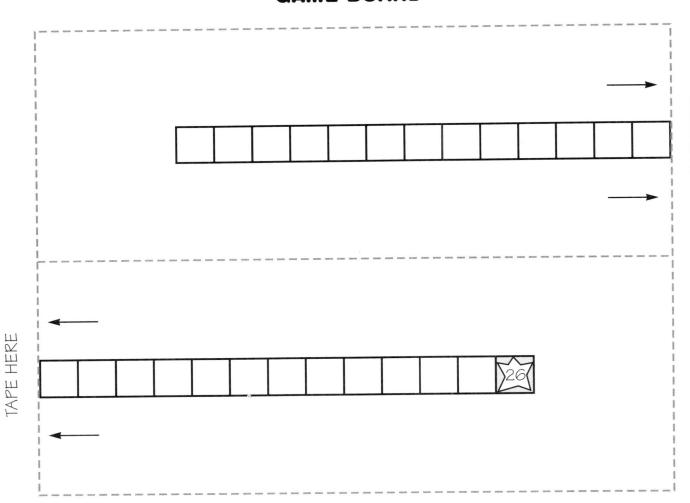

My scoopful had the following rods:

_____ white   _____ dark green

_____ red   _____ black

_____ light green   _____ brown

_____ purple   _____ blue

_____ yellow   _____ orange

I can trade my scoopful for _____ white rods.

Here is how I figured it out:

_____

_____

_____

_____

_____